Political Reasoning and Cognition

Political Reasoning and Cognition

A Piagetian View

Shawn W. Rosenberg, Dana Ward, & Stephen Chilton

DUKE UNIVERSITY PRESS   DURHAM AND LONDON 1988

© 1988 Duke University Press
All rights reserved
Printed in the United States of America
on acid-free paper ∞
Library of Congress Cataloging-in-Publication Data
appear on the last printed page of this book.

Contents

Preface

This is the long-awaited result of the collaborative effort of the three authors. The idea for the book was born at the 1982 meeting of the American Political Science Association where we discovered each other and our overlapping interests. Ward took the initiative and planned an edited volume to which Chilton and Rosenberg would contribute. This was completed in 1984. In response to the helpful suggestions of both Reynolds Smith of the Duke University Press and an anonymous reviewer, the project evolved into a coauthored effort by the three of us. Each of us took primary responsibility for writing different parts of the book. Despite this division of tasks, we all benefited from each other's constructive criticism. As might be expected, there are some important differences among us in how we interpret and use Piagetian theory. However, these are easily outweighed by a commonality of approach, one which we feel represents a challenge to current research and a fruitful direction for future efforts.

The general plan of the book is as follows. In this first chapter we offer a general introduction to the nature and relevance of a Piagetian approach to the study of politics. This extends both to a consideration of individuals' political attitudes and behavior and to reflections on the place of psychology in political theory. Throughout, we argue that psychological considerations are at the very core of political analysis.

Chapter two offers a critique of the current research on belief systems. The claim is made that while nearly thirty years of research has produced consistent results, the evidence offered ultimately tells us little about how people make sense of politics. As a solution, we suggest the need for a different conception of political thinking, one which builds on Piaget's developmental psychology. Following on this, chapter three provides an introduction to Piaget's theory of cognition. Piaget's work is presented as a powerful psychological theory, one which may importantly contribute to the study of political reasoning. The focus here is on the individual's reasoning as it develops from an initial egocentrism to a more sociocentric understanding of political events.

Chapters four and five develop Piaget's view further in the context of empirical research on political thought and ideology. Chapter four applies Piaget's analysis of egocentrism to the study of people's understanding of such basic political concepts as democracy and freedom. The results provide clear evidence of differences in political understanding among adults which correspond to Piagetian stages of cognitive development. Interestingly, the subjects who participated in this research are the grown children of the men used in Robert Lane's classic study, *Political Ideology*. Chapter five adopts a neo-Piagetian perspective and offers a somewhat different conception of political thinking. It sketches three types of political thinking and investigates the structural relationship between political and non-political thought. The focus here is on people's understanding of the American-Iranian hostage crisis of 1980. Drawing on experimental results as well as in-depth interviews, strong evidence is provided which suggests that there is an underlying structure to people's political reasoning and that this may vary from one adult to the next.

Chapter six and seven focus on macropolitical issues. Chapter six considers the implications of adopting a Piagetian point of view for the analysis of political culture. This leads to a redefinition of culture in terms which integrate meaning and action in a way distinct from, and yet relevant to, the analysis of individual's cognition. In so doing, the analysis provides new clarity and direction to this area of inquiry. Chapter seven offers a speculative analysis of power and political consciousness. As in chapter six, an attempt is made to reconceptualize these terms in light of a Piagetian understanding of reasoning and subjectivity. Chapters three, four and seven were written by Dana Ward. Chapter six was written by Stephen Chilton. I am responsible for chapters one and five and co-authored chapter two with Ward.

Taking a Piagetian Point of View

This book is a compilation of the efforts of three authors. While we focus on different issues, we all adopt the same basic approach—that of drawing on Piagetian theory to inform our analysis of politics. Guided by this approach, we address both micro-level questions pertaining to individuals' political thinking and macro-level ones regarding the implications of that thinking for the analysis of the polity. We explore a number of specific topics ranging from individuals' understanding of basic political concepts such as freedom and democracy to the implications of our concept of thinking for the analysis of political culture. Some of these studies are theoretical, others are empirical. Throughout, there is an attempt to offer a new perspective on political thought and action.

Apart from introducing our own particular theoretical perspective, we have two additional aims in writing this book. The first and most immediate is to broaden the purview of the empirical study of political thought and action. Too much attention has been paid to specific political attitudes and beliefs and too little to the understanding which underlies them. In an attempt to redress this imbalance, we present research which focuses on people's political understanding. Our second aim is to reintroduce a psychological dimension to political inquiry. Even when it focuses on individuals, current research retains an essentially sociological point of view. Individuals' political statements and acts are viewed with reference to their social or intersubjective definition and are explained with reference to social causes. In this book we focus on the subjective dimension of thought and action and argue that these must be both described and explained with reference to the individual. We also explore the implications of this view not only for the study of the individual, but for the analysis of the polity as well. In pursuing these aims, we hope to contribute to the search for new and better directions for political inquiry.

An Alternative Approach

Most contemporary research on political thinking focuses on people's political attitudes. In pursuing this course, it follows two complementary paths. On the one hand, it addresses the question of what people know about politics. Typically, people are asked to name officeholders such as the president or their member of congress or to list the responsibilities of particular institutions such as the Supreme Court or the State Department. On the other hand, the research examines people's feelings and preferences regarding these political entities. People are asked such questions as how warm or cold they feel about political leaders and to what extent they prefer one policy alternative to another. Taking the analysis a step further, researchers examine how these preferences are related to one another. Using more or less sophisticated statistical analyses, they assess the degree to which people's preference for one particular issue or candidate is correlated with their preferences for others.

In this book we adopt an alternative approach. It differs from most others in several basic respects. To begin, it poses a different question. Whereas the mainstream approach asks *what* people know and prefer, we ask *how* they know and prefer. Thus, we are interested in the reasoning people employ both to make sense of the particular facts they have at their disposal and to evaluate specific leaders and policies. This, in turn, leads to a consideration of the broader understanding of politics they construct. For example, if we are interested in studying people's awareness of American-Soviet relations, we do not end our inquiry by probing what it is people know about the actors involved and the specific actions they have taken. Instead, we probe further and pose such additional questions as: You have mentioned certain actors and institutions you believe to be involved; why are they involved and not others? You have mentioned certain things they have done; what else could they have been doing and why have they not pursued those alternative courses? Similarly, when conducting research on people's evaluation of American-Soviet relations, we do not simply ask whether American policies are good or bad. Rather, we begin with the person's evaluations and then ask questions designed to explore why the person believes that course is best, and further, why the justifications offered in response are pertinent or correct.

Our research also differs from most in its orienting conception of political thinking. Most contemporary research is concerned with the content of what people know about politics and want from it. Thus it becomes a matter of critical concern whether an individual identifies with the Republicans or the Democrats, or whether he or she favors an increase or decrease in defense spending. This focus on content is encouraged by the assumption of a shared understanding and its corollary, that the formal qualities of thinking are invariant. Even when the attention of researchers shifts from the substance of particular attitudes to the quality of the relationships among them, the concern with content remains fundamental. When distinguishing the general qualities of how different people think, the analysis focuses on the content of several attitudes at once and evaluates the degree to which that content matches the set of positions dictated by substantively defined ideologies. For example, researchers may consider one's views on welfare, government decentralization, and civil rights. To define the general quality of one's thought, they would then determine whether or not the set of views expressed matched that of a liberal or a conservative.

Interestingly, this strategy of categorizing types of thinking by matching content to ideal models has not worked particularly well. As clearly demonstrated in *The American Voter* (Campbell et al., 1960) and the work that followed, the attitudes of most individuals did not cluster in the way suggested by the ideal models. For the most part this somewhat anomalous finding was accounted for within the confines of a content-oriented definition of thinking.

Thus, the differences between people's attitudes and those of the ideal models (and later the differences among various individuals) were characterized with reference to the substance of their thinking. Perhaps the most influential expression of this approach is found in the typology proposed by Philip Converse (1964). Focusing on the content of their beliefs, Converse found that only a small percentage of people expressed attitudes which did correspond to either a liberal or a conservative cluster. Turning to the remaining 90 percent, he discovered that some were oriented to single issues, while others seemed to have no issue content to their thinking whatsoever. Converse differentiated among kinds of political thought as follows: (1) where the terms liberal or conservative are used in connection with specific beliefs conventionally associated with either ideology, (2) where the terms liberal or conservative are used in an incorrect or unconventional way, (3) where the focus is on group-related issues, (4) where the focus is on issues of war and peace or general economic well-being, (5) where there is no consideration of matters having any issue content. Consistent with the results of the correlational studies of policy preferences, Converse found that only a small percentage of people fell into the first category and almost half fell into the fourth and fifth categories.

In our research we acknowledge the aforementioned results, but this leads us to explore an alternative line of analysis, one largely ignored in the research literature. We claim that the apparent differences in the *content* of people's political attitudes may reflect (albeit obliquely) *formal* differences in how they think about and understand politics. In this vein we argue that people differ not only in the substance of their concerns, but also in the way they define, interrelate, and use specific information for the purpose of understanding and evaluating political events. Following this line, our research focuses on the nature of the relationships an individual constructs when thinking about political objects and on the quality of his or her definition of those objects.

For example, we are interested in whether an individual observing a flow of events understands it as a mere sequence of moments or as a series of causes and effects. Similarly, we are interested in determining whether an individual thinking about a governmental institution understands that institution as a single actor which does particular things or as an organizational system whose action is subject to both internal and external constraints.

Because we adopt a different theoretical point of view, we employ different research designs and methods from those commonly used in the research on political thought and behavior. The mainstream research assumes that at least within a single polity, people share a basic understanding of politics. This assumption underlies the logic of the commonly used methods and analytical strategies. For example, asking short-answer survey questions to explore people's political thinking makes sense only if it is assumed that all respondents (and the researcher) share the same basic understanding of the questions posed and the answers given. Similarly, the strategy of inferring the nature of individuals' thinking from an analysis of responses aggregated across individuals depends on the assumption that different respondents confer the same basic meaning on the statements they hear and make.

To illustrate, consider the use of the following question in an attempt to study the quality of people's attitudes toward their spouses: "Do you love your spouse? Please respond on a scale from 1 to 7." Such an approach is appropriate only if the term "love" has some common meaning for the people questioned and for the researcher. If it does not, the conclusions drawn by the researcher can only distort the realities. Imagine the result in a case where the respondents use the term as an empty rhetorical statement associated with the state of marriage and the researcher regards it as an indication of a complex of self- and other-oriented emotions. Similarly, a research design which involves aggregating many individuals' responses to the question in order to arrive at some general statement about the average spouse only makes sense if they all assign the same meaning to the term "love." If some assign the term an empty rhetorical meaning, and others view it as a conditional willingness to act on the behalf of another, and still others understand it to mean an unconditional feeling of certain emotions, it is clear that little will be gained by aggregating their responses.

In our work, understanding and meaning are regarded as objects of study rather than assumption. We begin by recognizing that people may reason differently and therefore come to understand the same events in very different ways. Consequently, we study each person individually. Rather than adopting the common strategy of considering a number of different people's responses to a single question, our research is designed so that we may examine a single person's responses to a number of different questions. When gathering data, we attempt to uncover the train of reasoning and the kinds of definitions the person uses when making sense of a particular question or problem. To do so we do not rely on closed-ended or short-answer questions. Rather, we pose open-ended problems and encourage the subject to respond at length. While more difficult to work with, these kinds of data are necessary if we intend to address the question of political understanding.

A Piagetian View of Thinking

Our theory and research draw heavily on those of Jean Piaget. Among political scientists, Piaget is well known but little used. The reason is straightforward. Political scientists know Piaget to be a developmental psychologist. Those who are aware of his work assume that it focuses on children and the stages they go through in the course of their intellectual maturation. While many may find this interesting in its own right, most regard it as irrelevant to political inquiry. After all, politics is the domain of adults, not children. Consequently, only those political scientists who study childhood political socialization have shown any interest in Piaget's work (e.g., Adelson, 1971; Adelson and O'Neil, 1966; Rosenau, 1975).

While there is a certain truth to this view, it entails a basic misunderstanding of Piaget's work and its possible relevance to political research. While focused on child development, the basic issue addressed in Piaget's theory and research is the nature of human thought. Conceiving this issue in its broadest terms, Piaget engaged in epistemological analysis as well as psychological research. Indeed, he regarded these two lines of inquiry to be intimately intertwined, the study of each depending on that of the other.

Genetic epistemology deals with both the formation and the meaning of knowledge. We can formulate our problem in the following terms: by what means does the human mind go from a state of less sufficient knowledge to a state of higher knowledge? . . . The fundamental hypothesis of genetic epistemology is that there is a parallelism between the progress made in the logical and rational organization of knowledge and the corresponding formative psychological process. (Piaget, 1970, pp. 12–13)

Thus, Piaget viewed his own efforts not only as an attempt to chart intellectual development, but more importantly as an effort to develop a general theory of thinking (Piaget, 1971a; 1971b). What we attempt in this volume is to build upon Piaget's research on children by extending the range of application in two directions: to adults and politics.

In our view it is as a general theory of thinking, one quite different from that adopted in most political research and theory, that Piaget's work will contribute to the study of politics. We extend his theory and use it to guide our studies of adult political thinking. The results of our research are presented in chapters four and five. Building on this, we also consider the implications of our view of adult political thinking for macropolitical analysis. In this light we offer a critical examination of current definitions of political culture and concepts of political power and put forward an alternative of our own. This is presented in chapters six and seven. It is important to note that in addressing these expressly political concerns we have importantly modified Piaget's theoretical position. Most important, we pay greater attention to the social dimension of the individual's construction of meaning.

In chapter three we provide a fully elaborated statement of Piaget's psychology. Here, we discuss several basic assumptions that guide both Piaget's and our own Piagetian research. One assumption is that thought is best conceived as an activity, as an operation on the world. Two points should be noted here. First, thought is not viewed in static terms, that is in terms of its constituent ideas or representations. Rather, it is viewed in dynamic terms, as the activity of thinking or reasoning. Viewed from this perspective, mental representations and ideas are phenomena of interest, but are of secondary concern. They are understood as derivative products of thinking. Second, thought is regarded as continuous with action in the real world. In basic respects thought and action are two manifestations of the same phenomenon: the individual's purposive attempt to operate on and in the world. Piaget's work, then, may be considered a continuation of a traditional focus on praxis which extends from Marx through American pragmatism.

A second basic assumption Piaget adopts is that thought is structured. The view here is that an individual has a basic capacity to think or reason. In the language of operations, an individual has a general way in which he or she is able to purposively act on the world. As the individual actually acts, this general capacity is realized in a variety of specific and concrete operations. It is substantively differentiated. For example, an individual may have a basic capacity to think in causal linear terms. Through actual experience, this capacity is realized in the specific connections the individual forges when thinking that if the government involves the military in the policing of the illegal drug trade, the level of drug abuse will decline, or that the decline of the British economy is a result of the laziness of the British laborer. While substantively quite distinct, these two understandings are structurally identical outcomes of the same kind of thinking or mode of operation. Thus, in Piaget's view, thinking, and the understanding it yields, are defined in formal terms and, at least in the first instance, are regarded as subjective acts. In this regard Piaget adopts concerns and strategies similar to those of continental structuralism. Like the structuralists, he assumes that there is a deep structure underlying the manifest content of human thought and that this content can be properly understood only with reference to its relation to that deep structure.[1]

The third basic assumption which distinguishes Piaget's perspective is that thought develops. This third postulate is best understood in relation to the preceding two and to a metaphysical assumption, largely implicit in Piaget's work, that reality itself is structured. The argument is that thinking is a subjectively structured attempt to

operate upon an objectively structured world. Insofar as the structure of an individual's thought is inconsistent with the structure of
the environment, his or her attempt to operate will prove unsuc-
cessful. Through a process of reflexive abstraction, a process of reflecting on how one thinks rather than simply focusing on the objects of one's thought, the structure of the individual's thought is
transformed. As a result of this process, the individual's thought is
transformed. The individual begins to operate in a new way on a
new kind of object, producing a new structure of thought. Consequently, thinking develops. Over time, this process generates a universal and invariant sequence of structural transformations, or
stages. For all individuals the starting point is the same—the re-
petoire of reflexes and perceptual ability that is common to the
species. The end is reached when the structure of the individual's
thought parallels that of reality.

In sum, Piaget adopts three basic assumptions: (1) thought is a
pragmatically constituted activity; (2) thought is structured; and (3)
thought develops. He orients his cognitive psychology accordingly.
For Piaget, the descriptive goal is to delineate the various forms
which thinking assumes in the course of its development. This involves describing the mode of thinking and the formal qualities of
the understanding constructed at each stage of development. Piaget
pursued this descriptive goal in two ways. In a series of book-length
analyses presented from the late 1920s through the 1940s, he attempted to establish the stages involved in the development of the a
priori categories of thought defined by Kant, such as causality, time,
and space. Ward's study of political concepts in chapter four follows
this approach. In his later work Piaget forged a more integrated
conception of the stages of development. Here, he attempted to
describe the general forms of operation which cut across the various
Kantian categories. This led to his definition of four general stages of
cognitive development. They are sensorimotor, preoperational, concrete operational, and formal operational thought. Although he defines these stages differently, Rosenberg adopts this approach in his
study of the general qualities of political thinking in chapter five.

The explanatory goal of Piaget's psychology is to explicate how
development occurs. He does so in complementary ways in the

course of his discussions of equilibration (the dynamic of adaptation of subjective to real structures) and reflexive abstraction. These discussions are, however, much more abstract and less elaborated than his analysis of the particular stages of development. Furthermore, little empirical research has been done to investigate these explanations. While such research was not conducted, it is not, in principle, impossible.[2]

Piaget's empirical research is designed with these goals in mind. The goal of describing the structural qualities of the various forms of thinking sets two guidelines for the design of descriptively oriented research. First, the investigation must focus on individual subjects. The possibility that different individuals may think in structurally dissimilar ways suggests that the common practice of using aggregate data to characterize typical performance is inappropriate. Second, the investigation must require each subject to perform several specific tasks. In this manner a content-free assessment of each subject's performance may more readily be made. Although little research has been conducted on the conditions of development, the design requirements are easily inferred. Individual subjects must be observed over time and, using quasi-experimental designs, an attempt must be made to examine the impact of differently structured environments on subjects' current thinking and long-term development. Chilton's examination of political cultures in chapter six establishes the framework for such a study in the political realm.

Piaget's methods, like his research designs, reflect the dictates of his concept of cognition. Given his assumption that thinking is structured and may vary across individuals, the methodological problems Piaget faced were quite similar to those of the historian of philosophy. The task confronting the historian of philosophy is to determine how a particular philosopher thinks. Aware that a philosopher may think in a quite distinctive way, the historian approaches the task of interpretation so as to avoid reducing the terms or logic of the philosopher's thought to his or her own. Viewed from a Piagetian perspective, people are lay philosophers with their own metaphysics and social theory. Like the historian of philosophy, the psychologist must attempt to build an interpretive model of the logic of people's thought. The psychologist, however, must begin by making subjects think in a way that can be observed. Recognizing that any single attitude or claim may mean different things to different people and therefore be easily misinterpreted, the psychologist uses empirical methods that give subjects the opportunity to make a set of related judgments or claims about a specific problem or issue. Methods of this kind include open-ended interviews and clinical experiments. Both methods involve the presentation of a problem to subjects and then a continual probing of their responses to allow for a clear determination of the nature of the connections they are making. Using these techniques, the psychologist ensures that the data collected are sufficiently rich—that each subject has made a sufficient number of related claims—to allow for the construction and/or testing of an interpretive model of that subject's thought.

To summarize, Piaget offers a distinctive approach to the study of human nature. He focuses on reasoning and the understanding it engenders. He defines reasoning as a structured pragmatic activity and explains the nature and development of structures of thought with reference to the general progress of intellectual development. His clinical experimental methods of psychological research complement this theoretical orientation. The result of his efforts is an extraordinary body of theoretical writings and empirical research on the nature and development of thinking. The significance of his contribution to psychology is widely recognized; but, again, its implications for political science have been explored only to a very limited degree.

Implications for Political Analysis

Piaget's view of thinking has important implications for the conduct of political science at a number of levels. Most obvious is its relevance for the study of public opinion. It suggests that this study focus on the individual's activity of reasoning about politics. Following this lead, we offer our Piagetian view of political ideology.

Our view of ideology is based on two key assumptions. The first is that ideological thought is structured and therefore constitutes a coherent whole. This structure and coherence are understood with reference to the nature of the activity of political reasoning. Like all reasoning, political reasoning consists of the individual's attempt to operate upon the world and then assimilate the results achieved. Thus, political reasoning provides the medium of exchange between the individual and the political environment. In so doing, it determines the structure of the individual's social and political experience. How the individual thinks (his or her capacity to operate and reflect) delimits both the nature of what the individual can experience (the quality of possible objects of thought) and the way in which the individual will organize those experiences (the type of analytical relations between objects established).

Our second basic assumption is that ideology develops. This development is a necessary result of the activity of political reasoning. Political reasoning is a fundamentally pragmatic activity; it is embedded in interaction with the environment and yields a guide to future interaction. Political reasoning thus provides the individual with a knowledge of how to act and what to expect. The individual directs future action and forms future expectations accordingly. In so doing, the individual relates his or her subjectively constructed ideology or political understanding to the realities of social and political life. Although the individual's action is subjectively structured and directed, it actually occurs in a socially structured environment. It is therefore necessarily regulated by the rules inherent in that sociopolitical environment. Given these social constraints on action, it is necessarily the case that the individual's ideology (as the guide to and reflection upon his or her own and others' action) will also necessarily be constrained by the structure of the environment.

The claim that political reasoning is socially as well as subjectively structured is critical to the developmental view of ideology. It is the interaction between these two structuring forces, subjective and social, which constitutes the developmental dynamic. To the extent to which the individual's ideological construction of political experience is inconsistent with the real constraints imposed on it by the environment, the individual's ideological understanding of the world will prove unworkable. This leads to reflection, a shift in focus from what one knows to how one knows. This in turn leads to the construction of a new structure of ideological thought. With reflection, the terms of the old ideological understanding are objectified and thereby transcended. The act of taking one's way of understanding as object prefigures the emergence of a new mode of political reasoning. With the application and consequent elaboration of this new mode of reasoning, the structure of ideology is transformed and political experience is reconstructed.

In sum, ideology is the result of an ongoing process of subjective construction, negation, reflection and reconstruction. This process has several distinctive characteristics. First, because each stage in the process both builds on the preceding stage and creates the foundation of the succeeding one, the order of development will not vary across persons. Second, because each stage emerges as a reflective response to the inadequacies of thought at the preceding stage, development leads both to an ever greater cognitive sophistication and to a more appropriate adaptation to the political environment. Third, because environments stimulate development, and the structure of environments may vary, different individuals may achieve different levels of development. These developmental differences will produce structural differences in reasoning and ideology across individuals.

It is important to note that our notion of social environments and their role in conceptual and ideological development goes well beyond Piaget's own thinking. Piaget saw participation in a social environment as essential to development. The requirements of participation in cooperative social interaction were regarded as critical pressures to develop higher-order thinking. However, this was conceived in only the broadest and vaguest sense. In Piaget's view, all social environments require some level of cooperative interaction. He did not suggest any cognitively relevant distinctions among forms of cooperative interaction. In this context it made little sense to investigate the relation between environments and forms of political thought.[3] We believe that the interactional structure of social environments does vary in a way that is relevant to the development of political thought. In Piagetian terms, we believe that there are different modes of social cooperation which place different cognitive developmental demands on the individuals involved. As we shall see in chapter five, this leads to a reconceptualization of the dynamic of development and the nature of the understanding achieved at each stage in its progress. An exemplary analysis of cognitively relevant differences in forms of social cooperation is presented by Chilton in chapter six.[4]

Accompanying this theory of ideology is a general program for empirical research. There are two orienting aims: (1) to characterize the various forms which political reasoning may take; and (2) to explain the conditions of the structural transformation of political reasoning. The first aim directs research to offer an account of the patterns in individuals' political arguments, evaluations, and judgments in terms of structures underlying their thought. The key concern here is the formal structure—the quality of the constituent relations and elements—of individuals' political thinking. Two points should be noted regarding this investigation of the quality of individuals' political thought. First, the emphasis on the analysis of the structure underlying the manifest content of individuals' political beliefs is not meant to suggest that particular beliefs are insignificant or impossible to study. They are likely to have important consequences in particular situations and are, therefore, significant. Our point here is that the meaning of a particular belief—and by implication its relation to other beliefs and external circumstances—is structurally delimited. Consequently, to study individuals' political beliefs, one must begin by having identified the structure which underlies their constitution and organization. Only in this context can analyses of the relations among beliefs and the conditions of specific attitude change be explored. Second, it should also be noted that this Piagetian program does not limit research to the study of thinking about only those phenomena which the culture defines as political. Central to any ideology is the definition of the boundaries of politics itself. Insofar as ideology is itself a subjective construction, the phenomena which constitute politics or are relevant to political belief are themselves subjectively determined. Thus, research must be guided by individuals' definitions, rather than cultural definitions, of what is political.

The second aim of our Piagetian research on ideology is to provide an account of how structures of political reasoning are transformed. Here, the focus is not simply on the individual but on the relationship between the individual and the polity, between subjective and intersubjective constitutions of politics. According to our view, political reason is constructed at different levels both by individuals and by the collectivity. The relationship between these two levels of structuration is dialectical: each is potentially transformed by virtue of its relation to the other. Consequently, changes in the structure of individuals' ideologies must be accounted for in terms of the structure of the sociopolitical environment to which the individual is exposed.

It is important to recognize that Piaget's perspective suggests more than just a theory of ideology or public opinion. It extends to a theory of political behavior as well. The key here is the theoretical definition of the relationship between thought and behavior. This relationship may be conceived in a variety of ways. Following the direction of attitude psychology, the mainstream research on political behavior presumes that thought (attitudes) is quite distinct from specific behavior, but that a close relationship exists between them. In this conception, attitudes direct behavior; they dispose an individual to behave in a particular way.[5] The problem with this conception, and with the implicit view of thought and behavior underlying it, is that it was not supported by empirical research. The problem was first noted in the social-psychological research. Put simply, attitudes do not predict behavior at all well.[6]

In the Piagetian view this social psychology of attitudes and behavior and its analog in political science depend on inappropriate concepts and therefore misconstrue central issues. Thought and behavior are not distinct, they are inextricably united in attempts to operate on the world, either through representation or observable action. Therefore, behavior, like thought, is purposive and subjectively structured on the one hand and is performed on objects and is constrained by the real conditions of thought and action on the other. The implication is that behavior must be viewed as subjectively defined action. Through the individual's interaction with the environment, the structure of this subjective definition develops. Therefore, to understand the meaning of a behavior—its inherent nature and relation to either attitudes or other behaviors—one must identify the subjective structure of the individual's political reasoning. Whereas in conventional research the problem is one of explaining behaviors in terms of attitudes or contexts, the key problem for a Piagetian investigation appears at a prior step—that of appropriately describing the behaviors or attitudes themselves in light of the structure that underlies them both. Only in this context can the investigator appropriately identify specific behaviors and attitudes and properly understand the relationships between them. Failure to proceed in this manner can result only in a potentially inappropriate and largely unself-conscious translation of an individual's behavior into the analyst's own terms of reference.

As a theory of individual thought and behavior, Piaget's work is also relevant to macropolitical analyses. All analyses of this kind are based on assumptions about individual thought and behavior. Indeed, these analyses make sense only if one accepts their underlying assumptions about how people understand (or fail to understand) institutional and social constraints. Piaget offers a very different concept of individual thought from that adopted in most contemporary political analyses. Consequently, his work constitutes a challenge to the psychological foundations of these analyses and therefore to the macropolitical theories built upon them.

To illustrate, let us briefly consider the implications of one aspect of the Piagetian view of cognition—the claim that among adults there are developmentally generated differences in reasoning. This claim runs contrary to the cognitive assumptions which underlie both liberal and sociological theories of politics. Although these two theories vary in their assessment of individuals' capacities, both assume that all individuals think in fundamentally the same way. Moreover, both types of macropolitical analysis depend on this assumption of common cognitive capacity.

Consider first the liberal view of human nature and politics. According to this view, all individuals share a common capacity to reason. Some people may be quicker or more knowledgable than others, but all share the same basic capacity for rational thought. The centrality of this assumption is readily apparent when considering the liberal conception of a political institution. An institution is defined by the ways in which it regulates the interaction among citizens. Examples include various governmental institutions, the laws they create, and the policies they pursue. Key to the liberal conception of any institution is that all individuals appreciate the regulatory imperatives of the institution similarly and respond in a comparable fashion. It is in this context that it is possible to conceive *the* institution in question. The singularity of its identity depends on its common impact and realization in day-to-day activity. The liberal assumption of a common rationality assures this. The only qualification is that individuals share comparable exposure to the same basic information.

In this regard the sociological view of politics is not very different. Individuals are regarded as less able, but, like the liberal view, it is assumed that they all have the same basic cognitive capacity. According to the sociological view, all individuals share the same capacity to perceive environmental stimuli and to associate rewards with various responses. Again, this micro-level assumption is critical to macro-level conceptualization. Central to the sociological view of politics is the assumption that society is a structured, coherent entity. It defines an interactive or organizational framework which shapes politics. While an extraindividual or collective phenomena, this social organization is ultimately manifest in the behavior of individuals. It must define their goals and direct their action. It does so through a process of socialization. Critical to this view is the assumption that all individuals have the same basic capacity to perceive and learn the role requirements imposed on them by their place in this social organization. This insures that all will recognize and respond in the same designated manner. In this context, it is reasonable to refer to the single collective organization of individuals' action.

The Piagetian view of cognition denies the validity of the assumption that all individuals think in basically the same way. To the contrary, it suggests that they may perceive, reason, and comprehend in fundamentally different ways. By denying the assumption of common cognition, the Piagetian view implies the need for a basic reconceptualization of both liberal and sociological views of politics. The assumption of individual differences in cognitive processing suggests that the same objective environment will be understood differently and therefore responded to differently by different individuals. In the liberal case this implies that a given institution's regulatory initiatives will be understood and responded to according to a variety of logics. The intersubjective agreement as to the nature of the institution is lost. Therefore, it does not make sense to refer to *the* institution because in fact there are several, each with its own subjectively mediated definition and behavioral realization. The implications for the sociological view are similar. Insofar as individuals vary in their capacity to perceive stimuli and rewards and to relate them to each other, it makes no sense to talk about a single organizational framework or culture which determines their interaction. There is no common perception which assures the singular realization of an objective phenomenon such as social structure. Differences in the subjective mediation of objective phenomena suggest that multiple organizational frameworks may be operative in a single objectively defined social setting.

In sum, the Piagetian assumption of individual differences in cognition raises fundamental questions regarding both liberal and sociological theories of politics. At stake is both theories' assumption that the polity or society is a coherent entity and hence an appropriate object of theoretical analysis. The Piagetian claim of structural differences in individuals' reasoning denies the common subjectivity which underlies the liberal assumption of intersubjective agreement and the sociological assumption of a common perception. In so doing, it suggests that the polity or a society is not a coherent, single entity, but rather a loose confederation of occasionally overlapping patterns of exchange which are best described and explained at a more local level of analysis. In coming to this conclusion, we see how Piagetian theory, a psychology, pertains to macropolitical analysis. It offers theory and evidence on individuals from which we may deduce the nature of interpersonal exchange and possible forms of political organization.

Of course, Piagetian theory provides not only a basis for criticism, it also suggests new directions for political theory. With its emphasis on structural developmental analysis, Piagetian theory builds on an epistemology which favors an interpretive analysis of patterns of action and an explanation of those patterns with reference to underlying structures. In this respect it is sympathetic to the general theoretical orientation of much sociological analysis. At the same time Piaget places the locus of structure in the individual, regarding structure as a cognitive phenomenon; in this regard his theory stands in opposition to sociological analysis. The inherent tension in these twin considerations delineates the direction for political theorizing. It calls for a truly social psychological conception of political life, one which realizes the full ramifications of the claim that politics is at once an individual and a collective phenomenon.

Attitude, Belief, and Ideology:
The Need for New Directions

Empirical research depends on concepts and theory. No matter how careful the methods and sophisticated the statistical analysis, research can be no better than the theory which directs it. Although regarded as truisms, these simple claims generally receive little more than lip service. For the most part, reviews of empirical research focus on technical issues of data collection and analysis and ignore larger questions of conceptualization. This is frequently the case even when the results of the research are confusing and the ensuing methodological critique and tinkering fail to yield a satisfactory understanding. As a result, one of the key aims of empirical research, the challenging of prevalent theory, is blocked. Theory and research become separated from one another and both suffer.

In our view current efforts to study political ideology are significantly undermined by this separation of theory and research. The empirical study of ideology has reached something of a crisis. Established findings are being called into question and new directions are needed. Unfortunately, debate has revolved around questions of method. Little attention has been devoted to a consideration of the fruitfulness of the concepts employed and the adequacy of the basic theory which underlies them. Here, we redirect attention to these more fundamental questions. In so doing we conclude that the belief systems research is confronted by questions it cannot solve, and we suggest that a new framework for analysis is needed.

We begin with a review of the mainstream of the empirical research on ideology. We conclude that this research fails to offer either a comprehensive or unambiguous view of how people think about political phenomena. To explain this failure, we consider the theory underlying the research. We focus on the concept of the structure of political thinking at the heart of that theory and question its adequacy. We conclude that future research requires a new theory to guide the development of both basic concepts and empirical methods.[1]

Ideology as Belief System

The empirical study of political thought and ideology has been dominated by a belief systems approach. This is particularly true in the United States and Britain. Although it has been adopted by a large number of researchers over the last thirty years, the approach has been most influentially developed in the work of Philip Converse (e.g., Converse's contribution in Campbell et al., 1960; Converse, 1964, 1975). Converse defines political thinking in terms of the particular preferences that individuals express regarding the political issues and candidates of the day.[2] The meaning of a preference or belief is not itself viewed as problematic. Rather, it is assumed that beliefs have some objective or intersubjective meaning which is readily accessible to the culturally informed observer. In this context the key concern becomes one of establishing how beliefs are associated with one another in larger systems of belief. These systemic associations are themselves explicated with reference to the concept of constraint. In dynamic terms this constraint suggests that the relations among beliefs are regulated so that when one belief changes, other related beliefs also change. In more static terms this suggests that beliefs are related to one another according to specific determinations of the associative (implicatory) or dissociative (contradictory) connections which exist between them.

To explain how particular beliefs are associated with one another in a belief system, Converse delineates three possible sources of constraint: logic, psychological tendencies, and societal definition. Converse does not regard the first source of constraint, logic, to be a particularly significant force in the thinking of the average individual. The second, psychological pressures resulting from a person's experience of what beliefs seem to be properly associated with what other beliefs, is regarded as important. However, Converse emphasizes how this experience is itself shaped by the political environment to which the individual is exposed. Consequently, it is societal definitions that are seen to be the most critical factor in the organization of an individual's political beliefs. In this regard the belief systems approach adopts a loose learning theory view of socialization. It is assumed that the individual's social environment provides information on which aspects of political life are deserving of attention, how these aspects are to be evaluated, and how they stand in relation to one another. Through exposure to this information, the individual learns about politics and organizes his or her beliefs accordingly.[3]

The methods of gathering data employed in the belief systems research reflect the foregoing conception of political thinking. Data on political thinking are collected through the administration of a survey. Subjects are presented a number of closed-ended questions which ask them to express their policy preferences and their attitudes toward political candidates. In addition, subjects are generally asked a few open-ended questions. Here, they are given the opportunity to briefly justify their views of the leading presidential candidates and the two major political parties. While some of the belief systems research focuses on these more unwieldy short-answer items, the bulk relies on an analysis of the closed-ended ones. In either case the overwhelming majority of the work depends on the data gathered on national samples by one or two survey research centers.

Given the conceptual framework they adopt and the kind of data they collect, Converse and those following his lead have tended to adopt three analytical strategies for exploring the nature of belief systems. The one which is perhaps most consistent with his definition of a belief system entails the statistical analysis of the interrelationships among responses to survey items. This involves the examination of the average intercorrelation of pairs of items coded along a liberal-conservative continuum. Here again there has been some debate. A number of researchers have argued that the dimensions around which belief systems are organized should not be presumed by the researcher. Therefore, rather than imposing the liberal-conservative dimension on the data as Converse does, his critics have relied on various factor-analytic techniques to enable whatever dimensions structure belief systems to emerge from an analysis of the data (Luttbeg, 1968; Jackson and Marcus, 1975; Stimson, 1975; Judd and Milburn, 1980; Himmelweit et al., 1981).[4]

The second line of analysis focuses on the stability of the individual's attitudes. Here the reasoning is that insofar as the individual does have a belief system, the attitudes which constitute it should remain relatively stable over time. To test attitude stability Converse has relied on test-retest correlations for specific survey items. Both his focus on attitude stability and his measure of that stability have been subject to criticism. Himmelweit has raised the problem that salience and meaning of specific issues change over time and, therefore, one should not expect attitudes toward them to remain stable (Himmelweit et al., 1981). Others have criticized Converse's statistical analyses for failing to account adequately for such factors as measurement error (Achen, 1975) and the variety in possible sources of attitude change (Judd and Milburn, 1980).

The third line of analysis pursued by Converse involves the content analysis of the short answers to questions requiring political candidate and party evaluations. This analysis constitutes an attempt to complement the analysis of inter-item correlations with a direct investigation of the principles governing the individual's belief system. Based on the content analysis of their responses, subjects are divided into five groups: ideologues (those who correctly employ the terminology of liberalism and conservatism); near-ideologues (inappropriate use of the terminology); group-interested (group loyalty mediates preferences); nature of the times (some issue content but no apparent organizing principle); and no issue content (Converse, 1964). Slightly different categories have been developed in subsequent research (e.g., Field and Anderson, 1969; Nie et al., 1976). Debate here has centered on whether the analysis does successfully capture how people think or whether it only measures the political rhetoric people use (Wray, 1979; Smith, 1980).

It is important to remember that these debates over Converse's methods and analysis have been conducted largely within the conceptual parameters defined by Converse. Therefore, researchers involved in these debates have not questioned Converse's empirical aims and basic research strategies. Instead, they have questioned the adequacy with which these aims and basic strategy have been operationalized in specific instances. For example, one popular line of attack has been to draw on Converse's claim that reasoning is an externally mediated process and then to argue that certain aspects of his survey items or analytical procedure fail to adequately account for the immediate or remote externalities influencing the subjects' responses (e.g., bias in the wording of questions, inappropriate characterization of the culturally defined dimensions around which beliefs are organized, and failure to adequately account for environmental change in the assessment of attitude stability).

In sum, despite some methodological controversy, the broad outlines of Converse's research strategy remain intact. Virtually all the research, including that currently being conducted, relies on surveys for data and analyzes those data by examining inter-item relationships, response stability over time, and the content of short answers.

What then has been the result of this apparently rather cohesive research effort? Relying on the concepts and methods described above, researchers have produced a considerable body of evidence on political belief systems. Needless to say, the methodological debates have produced controversy over some results. Nonetheless, a certain pattern, one suggested by Converse, does emerge. The evidence produced by Converse and those following in his tradition have yielded the following conclusions: (1) that the belief systems of most people are *not* well constrained (low inter-item correlations), are *not* stable (low test-retest correlations), and are *not* principled (low percentage categorized ideological); (2) that masses are less sophisticated than elites; and (3) that the degree of organization evidenced by the belief systems of mass publics is influenced somewhat by the political climate of the times. Pointing to issues of question construction and analytical technique, Converse's critics have raised questions about the appropriateness of all three conclusions. In the main, however, it appears that the overall impact of their criticism has been to add a note of caution rather than to reverse the conclusions drawn by Converse and his supporters.

In sum, the main thrust of Converse's statement remains intact after more than twenty-five years of research. His methods, with some technical improvements, continue to be employed in current research. Even his initial conclusions remain accepted by most scholars in the field. Thus, our review of the belief systems research suggests that despite some methodological debate, researchers are oriented by a shared set of concepts which have produced reasonably durable results. Consequently, we might regard the belief systems research effort as a success.

Reassessing the Research

In our view to call the belief systems research effort a success would be premature. A closer consideration of the evidence leads us to make the following claims: (1) in fact, we know very little about how the mass of people reason about politics; and (2) what little we do know stands on very uncertain ground. We shall discuss each claim in turn.

Our claim that we know very little about how people reason about politics is based on a consideration of how much of the mass public's beliefs is captured by the research. A brief review of the research on levels of conceptualization and inter-item correlations indicates that very little is accounted for by the results.

In the case of levels of conceptualization, only 2.5 percent (Converse, 1964) to 6 percent (Klingemann, 1973) to 30 percent (Nie et al., 1976, 1979) of the population seem to think about politics along ideological lines which are readily interpretable. Very little can be said about the overwhelming majority, including about 30 to 40 percent who appear to be oriented to the concerns of one group or another, or the remainder, who either use ideological terms in an inappropriate or uninterpretable fashion or exhibit no apparent organization to their beliefs whatsoever. If we accept the data, the suggestion is that we can make clear sense of the understandings and orientation of somewhere between 2.5 percent and 30 percent of the population and less clear sense of an additional 30 to 40 percent. All we can say about the remainder is that they do not think along lines defined by our concepts. We can make little claim to knowing how they do think.

A similar problem emerges when we examine the research on inter-item correlations. Here the problem is that the model accounts for little of the variation in responses. Looking just at the most favorable case, inter-item correlations among assessments of domestic issues, the amount of variance explained varies from a mere 4 percent in the worst of times (late 1950s; Converse, 1964) to 25 percent in the best of times (Nie et al., 1976, 1979). This means that these correlational analyses fail to account for anywhere from 75 to 96 percent of the variance in beliefs about domestic issues—the very domain of thought in which this analytical conception has proved most descriptive of actual behavior. This suggests that the conception of political thinking underlying the correlational analysis allows us to make sense of only a small proportion of the political beliefs of mass publics.

In this context we should note the work of those researchers who have suggested that the inter-item correlational analysis be abandoned. Rather than imposing any theoretically defined structure on the data, these researchers have suggested that empirical research be used to discover the dimensional structure of belief systems. Using various kinds of factor analytical techniques, these researchers have discovered a number of factors—anywhere from one (Judd and Milburn, 1980) to five (Luttbeg, 1968; Himmelweit et al., 1981) to six (Kerlinger, 1984) to seven (Jackson and Marcus, 1975)—which enable them to account for about half of the variance in responses. Given that these dimensions are generated from the data rather than being theoretically identified, it is surprising how little of the variance is accounted for. These a posteriori accounts fail to describe half of the variance in the very data upon which those accounts are based.

The research on levels of conceptualization and inter-item correlations has led political scientists to conclude that mass publics tend not to have constrained belief systems. In our opinion this conclusion tells only half, and perhaps the least significant half, of the story. The other conclusion to be drawn from the evidence is that the research on political belief systems tells us very little about how most people think about politics.

While our first line of criticism suggests that research on belief systems tells us very little, our second line of criticism addresses that little bit which it does tell us. In this regard we take a closer look at the interpretability of the positive evidence which has been gathered.

Consider first the evidence on inter-item correlations. While the lack of correlation gives us no insight into how attitudes might be organized, at least the presence of strong correlation should give us that information. Upon closer consideration, however, it is not at all clear that evidence of correlation among attitudes tells us very much.

Let us consider the example of a subject who responds quite favorably to survey items A and B. What does this tell us about the relationship between A and B? The answer is that the information offered is ambiguous because the subjective meaning of the relationship is uncertain. It may be that the subject holds attitude A and attitude B, but does not forge any subjective link between them. Alternatively, the subject may hold attitude C and have learned that A is associated with C and B is associated with C. In this case links are forged, but the subjective meaning of these links is unclear. Finally, it may be that the subject has a general view X which defines his or her orientation to the specific attitudes A and B. In this case the subject understands A and B as members of a common class. Which of these three alternatives truly characterizes the connection underlying the correlation cannot be determined.

What are the consequences of this ambiguity? The direct consequence is that we cannot be sure of the subjective meaning of the relationship between the beliefs correlated. Thus, we cannot describe how the subject is thinking. The indirect consequence of this ambiguity is that whatever descriptions we do offer will not give us any conceptual leverage. Because the evidence does not allow us to interpret the meaning of the link between beliefs, we cannot determine the source of constraint. Therefore, we cannot go beyond the specific data in hand to predict other attitudes the subject may hold or how the subject would respond to a novel situation.

It should be noted that the factor analytic studies of attitude structure offer us no more than the simple correlational analyses. Indeed, they offer us less. At least the interitem correlations are based on a theoretically defined dimension and, therefore, some interpretation of relationships (even if inappropriate) is possible. In the case of the factor analytic studies, no such theoretical definition of dimensions exists, and the researcher is left trying to make some post factor sense of the factors which do emerge. This problem is exacerbated by the fact that the configuration of factors will vary with the kinds and number of attitude items used (for example, see Judd and Milburn, 1980; Stimson, 1975; Himmelweit et al., 1981; Jackson and Marcus, 1975). One may reasonably question the meaningfulness and the utility of an analysis in which the definition of dimensions depends both on the interpretive whim of the individual researcher and on the specific combination of survey items used to build the factor model.

The problem of the interpretation of the data also arises in the research on levels of conceptualization. While it is true that the open-ended question format gives the subject greater opportunity to reveal his or her sense of the issues, the problem of interpreting the meaning of the concerns voiced and the nature of their interrelation remains. The difficulties here are that subjects generally do not offer sufficient elaboration of their claims and justifications to allow for confident interpretation, and that interviewers are not sufficiently sensitive to the requirements of interpretation to probe as required. Thus, even in the most favorable circumstances, where the data appear quite comprehensible and are being directly examined by a coder, interpretation remains uncertain.

For example, consider the case in which the coder is confronted with responses such as the following. "I like Ted Kennedy." "Why?" "Well, I tend to be pretty liberal, and so is he. I mean who wants a President who isn't concerned with the poor and just wants to protect the rich from taxation." While it appears that the respondent is an ideologue, can we be sure? Is there sufficient evidence to conclude that his thought is mediated by some abstract liberal principle regarding the role of government in society? Why not assume that the respondent views liberals as a group, identifies himself with this group, and has learned the set of views that liberals hold? In fact, we lack sufficient data to choose between the two interpretations and must conclude that no satisfactory conclusion can be drawn. Remember that this is a result of a reasonably clear case. In this light, we must be even more suspicious of the interpretations of data which are less certain, by virtue of either the nature of the response given or the manner in which the data are interpreted (word identification using master codes as in Field and Anderson, 1969, and Nie et al., 1976).[5]

It appears, then, that the open-ended questioning and the content analyses used in the research on levels of conceptualization do not yield data which can be interpreted with any confidence. Failing to sufficiently probe the subject's sense of his or her own claims, the research does not afford any insight into what the subject is thinking. It cannot be determined whether the subjects' responses are rhetorical or reasoned and, if the latter, what the nature of the reasoning is. Failing to offer sufficient evidence for interpreting the meaning of subjects' responses, the research cannot offer an adequate basis for determining the conditions under which those responses will be maintained or altered. When researchers do predict the stability of subjects' responses (Converse, 1964, 1975), they will most probably fail (Smith, 1980).

Considering both the research which relies on the correlation analysis of inter-item relationships and the research which relies on content analysis of open-ended, short-answer questions, it is apparent that the little positive evidence on political belief systems is largely uninterpretable. Consequently, the conclusions based on that evidence must be considered with some skepticism.

In sum, our reconsideration of the research on political belief systems leads us to draw two conclusions: (1) that the research offers little information on how most people reason about political phenomena; and (2) what information is offered must, at best, be considered to be of uncertain status. Put simply, the data on political belief systems are not very good.

Understanding the Problem:
A Question of Theory

In our view the limitations of the belief systems research are not a matter of method. They are inherent in the concepts guiding that research. Most problematic is the link between the structure of thinking, on one hand, and constraint among beliefs on the other. In the belief systems research the concepts of constraint and structure are intimately intertwined. Constraint is evidence of structure and structure explains constraint. More profoundly, structure is defined in terms of constraint. Indeed, it is not explicated in any other terms. In what follows, we offer several criticisms of the link between structure and constraint.

The key failing in the equation of constraint among beliefs with the structure of political thinking is the resulting confusion of content and form. Constraint among beliefs must ultimately be defined in particular terms, that is with regard to what particular beliefs appear in conjunction with what others. Left undetermined is the form of this conjunction, that is, how the beliefs are related. Consequently, little attention is paid to how people understand the beliefs they express. It is in this context that we understand why the belief systems research has failed to generate an unambiguous description of how most people think about politics.

The need to define the structure of thinking independent of its content first became a critical issue for the political behavior research in the debates revolving around *The Authoritarian Personality* (Adorno et al., 1950). Rokeach noted in the introduction to *The Open and Closed Mind* (1960) that "a first requirement, it seems to us, is to make a sharp distinction between the structure and the content of ideological systems" (p. 14). Discussing studies of authoritarianism, he points out that holding all the "correct" liberal, anti-McCarthy, anti-racist, pro-Jewish beliefs does not automatically make a person nonauthoritarian, for those beliefs can be held in an authoritarian manner. In his view these studies are seriously flawed because they focus on *what* is believed, not *how* it is believed.

Although Rokeach applies his "first requirement" to studies of authoritarianism and dogmatism, we argue that any study of thought and belief must attempt to separate structure from content. We have demonstrated some of the consequences of failing to do so. There is, however, another macro-level consequence, the creation of a deep cultural bias in research. Researchers lack any formal or abstract concept of ideology. They are therefore forced to consider the specific content of the beliefs espoused by a given population of individuals. As a result, their definition of ideology necessarily reflects the cultural bias of that population.

This point underlies the criticism of the belief systems research done by Robert Lane and Lance Bennett. Both have argued that the repeated finding of differences in the structure of elite and mass belief systems is an artifact of the way constraint is defined. Lacking a formal definition of ideological structures, researchers focus on the particular associations among beliefs evidenced by a political elite. In their words:

> First, there has been a tendency to view the purported mode of belief organization among elites as the *only* meaningful way to organize beliefs. This makes the . . . argument both transparent and tautological. Secondly, the perceived exclusivity of universal dimensions of judgment has led investigators to measure attitude constraint in the mass public in such a way that other modes of attitude and belief organization would not be detected even if they existed. (Bennett, 1975, p. 9)

Further: "The mistake underlying reliance on the constraints implied by statistical clustering, scalar ordering, or acceptance of an idea cluster by an authoritative elite is based on the fallacious view that if some people see idea elements properly clustering in a certain way, others should too. Such 'constraints' or clusterings refer to neither logic nor rationality" (Lane, 1973, p. 103).

Consider the following illustration of their point. A given citizen might argue in favor of disarmament, reduced arms sales to Third World countries, *and* military aid for the Afghan insurgents. Seen against the backdrop of current American politics, such a collection of attitudes might appear to be a random cluster of otherwise disconnected beliefs. However, a wholly rational and well-considered process of judgment may in fact be at work. All three positions are compatible with just war theory (e.g., Walzer, 1977) and principles of self-determination. The point here is that if we assume that there is a single or small set of cultural "blueprints" for "what goes with what" and consequently do not assess the how and why of people's thinking, we will not discover the myriad ways in which people make sense of their world. Often we will see only nonsense where in fact a clear personal sense does exist.

The problem extends beyond the domain of comparing American masses and elites. It implies that the belief systems research lacks the requisite conceptual basis for the conduct of sensible cross-cultural research. The problem here becomes clear if we imagine the difficulties one would encounter in trying to compare the structure of beliefs in the United States with the structure of beliefs in Nepal, Chad, and Peru. Even if we were able to overcome problems of translation and question wording we could hardly be certain that liberalism and conservatism (or any other content-based analysis) meant the same things or were even relevant to these diverse cultures.

A similar problem arises in historical research. Culture is bound by time as well as space. Cultural differences for a given society across time may be as great as those which exist across societies. In both cases, analyses of the "structure" of belief systems using constraint as the measure of structure are limited to the circumstances of their origin, to the culture and historical moment of the population first studied. Unbiased cross-cultural comparison is possible only if there is a psychologically rooted and formal definition of structures of ideological thought. Only under this condition can we hope to construct a universally applicable concept and measure.

Beyond its confusion of form and content, the equation of the structure of political thinking with constraint is inadequate in a second respect: it limits the consideration of thinking to only one of its aspects. Constraint corresponds to only one of the many cognitive operations which produce a structured belief system. That is the operation of class inclusion. The set of liberal and conservative beliefs which are constrained are simply particular members of the general class of liberalism or conservatism. That class can be structured in many different ways. The point here is that the cognitive operations which produce a structured belief system are far more numerous, and in many ways far more important (at least in terms of their potential impact on political behavior) than mere class inclusion.

For example, Piaget held reversibility to be among the last and most critical cognitive operations to develop. The development of reversibility marks the watershed between concrete and operatory thought. In the political sphere an individual can hold a set of liberal beliefs which are either concrete or operatory, but that structure could not be detected simply by ascertaining the presence or absence of particular issue positions. One would have to determine whether or not the individual could move from general principles to particular applications *and* back again before a judgment could be made on the nature of the belief structure. Such reversibility, then, is essential to a structural analysis. Other types of cognitive operations (besides class inclusion and reversibility) that certainly ought to be included in a structural analysis of ideology are differentiation, identity, causality, seriation, transitivity, role-taking, and conservation. Again, the point is that by limiting the concept of structure to class inclusion we have too narrowly constricted the cognitive foundation upon which the structure of a belief system is built.[6] We have thereby closed off vast areas of further research.

The Need for an Alternative

Given our conclusions, what inferences do we draw? What course do we follow in order to formulate a more fruitful line of inquiry? In answering these questions it is important to remember two points. First, the evidentiary problems identified arose both across the variety of methods employed in the research and, where there was methodological debate, in the research alternative provided by either side. Second, both the various methods used in the research and the concepts they were intended to investigate constitute a cohesive framework and reflect a particular view of human understanding. In this light we suggest that our critique must not be viewed with reference to any particular method or concept. Instead, it should be regarded with reference to the general methodological orientation characteristic of the belief systems research and the conceptual framework which underlies it.

Examining this framework, we considered one of its core assumptions, that of the equation of the structure of thinking with the evidence of constraint among its contents, and found it lacking. It entails a confusion of form and content which leads to cultural bias in research, elitism in national studies, and parochialism in cross-cultural and historical studies. Therefore, we suggest that: (1) the utility of existing approaches to the study of belief systems be called into question; and (2) an alternative approach, one based on a clear distinction between the form and content of thinking, be developed.

Genetic Epistemology: A Piagetian Analysis of Political Thought

In chapter two we reviewed the concepts and methods employed in the belief systems research and emphasized that those conducting this research share the same basic approach. Underlying this approach is a certain understanding of the fundamental character of human knowledge and learning. This understanding is based on the epistemological perspective articulated by John Locke and later developed by David Hume, Bertrand Russell, and Gilbert Ryle. Central to this perspective are two assumptions: (1) reasoning consists of an awareness of particular phenomena and determination of the relations that exist among them—thus, reasoning is a subjective process which is mediated by objective circumstances; and (2) all individuals reason in fundamentally the same way—some individuals may be quicker, some smarter, and some more educated, but they all perceive and process information similarly.

These two assumptions structure the basic concepts and approach of the belief systems research. It is because of the implicit assumption that reasoning involves an awareness of objects and their interrelationships that it makes sense to view political thinking as consisting of individual attitudes (defined in part by the objects to which they refer) which may be related to one another in a system of beliefs. This also makes it appropriate to assume that the nature of an individual's belief system will reflect the configuration of infor-

mation to which he or she is exposed. This second assumption regarding the universal quality of human reasoning also justifies the
view that all people share the same basic understanding of information presented to them and confer the same basic meaning on the
beliefs they express. Differences may emerge, but these consist only
of particular differences in how given objects are evaluated or in
how specific attitudes are associated with one another. Referring
back to the first assumption, these differences in belief are explained
with reference to differences in the social environments and up-
bringing which individuals have experienced.[1]

In contrast to this Lockean view, Piaget's epistemology is Kantian, albeit in the same sense that Marx's epistemology is Hegelian.
That is, just as Marx turned Hegel on his head, Piaget has turned
Kant on his head by arguing that the structures of thought are not
innate but are actively constructed through interaction with the
environment. Hence, Piaget shares with Kant a belief in the a priori,
but the a priori stands at the end of a process of development; it is
not given initially. Knowledge is not merely a reflection of reality,
or a product of the epistemic subject, but the product of their interaction such that subject and object become indissociable. But
already we are ahead of ourselves. Before we can fully appreciate the
differences between the essentially Lockean epistemology which
presently dominates belief systems research and the essentially
Kantian epistemology which we propose as a substitute, let us take
a closer look at the work of Jean Piaget.

Piaget and the Development of Knowledge

As we noted earlier, most people familiar with the name Jean Piaget
think of him as a child psychologist. Even people who might have
read one or two books by Piaget, either in undergraduate psychology
courses or in graduate education courses, would most likely agree
with that categorization. It is by no means an illogical conclusion
given that Piaget authored no fewer than seventeen books that bear
in their titles the words "child," "children," or "childhood." To call
Piaget a child psychologist, however, is to miss the major thrust of
his monumental work. Although a biologist by training, Piaget

would have preferred the discipline he practiced to be described as "genetic epistemology." Indeed, all the studies of childhood cognitive development were conducted in order to provide the underpinnings of this new discipline which he founded. The first step in understanding Piaget, then, is to place his work in the context of genetic epistemology. We can then contrast genetic epistemology with the epistemology which currently informs the analysis of belief systems in political science.

Piaget's opening sentence in *Genetic Epistemology* bears repeating: "Genetic epistemology attempts to explain knowledge, and in particular scientific knowledge, on the basis of its history, its sociogenesis, and especially the psychological origins of the notions and operations upon which it is based" (p. 1). This statement should make it clear that the purpose of the cognitive studies was to uncover the psychological foundations of scientific knowledge. Piaget's focus was on the ways in which real human thought becomes capable of producing scientific knowledge and, again, he expressed the "fundamental hypothesis" of genetic epistemology as follows: "There is a parallelism between the progress made in the logical and rational organization of knowledge and the corresponding formative psychological processes" (p. 13). In short, Piaget *de*constructed the mechanisms of human knowledge in order to answer the central question of epistemology: how does human thought produce scientific knowledge?

We might stop here and ask what possible relevance all this has for political science. If the foregoing analysis of the concept of structure used in political science is even remotely on target, then it is clear that we are in need of an epistemologically grounded set of analytical categories if we are ever to be reasonably sure that our descriptions of belief systems are at all meaningful, let alone communicable across disciplines in the social sciences. As an example of the potential power of clarification that genetic epistemology has for political science, we might look at a field even more remote from cognitive development than political beliefs: physics.

Piaget first studied the development of the child's conception of time and speed at Einstein's suggestion. Piaget was particularly fond of recounting the role that these studies played in clarifying certain problems for two physicists attempting to provide an axiomatization of Einstein's theory of relativity. Their problem was the need to avoid the vicious circle in the relationship between speed and time. Some years after Piaget's initial studies the two physicists chanced upon his work, and as a result they were able to introduce into their system independent notions of time and speed based on the ordinal notion of speed Piaget had discovered in his studies of children.

Extending the example to political science, we argue that the discipline can benefit by adapting Piaget's analysis of the transformations of thought in general to the transformations of political beliefs in particular. For example, if we can document the ontogenic sequences through which political concepts develop, then we will have an empirical basis for judging the degree to which mass beliefs are more or less structured.

The mechanisms by which thought is transformed are the basics of genetic epistemology. The purpose of the transformation is to provide more adequate knowledge, and genetic epistemology studies the ways in which the transformations move an individual from less adequate to more adequate systems of knowledge: "Genetic epistemology deals with both the formation and the meaning of knowledge. We can formulate our problem in the following terms: by what means does the human mind go from a state of less sufficient knowledge to a state of higher knowledge?" (Piaget, 1970, p. 12). The answer Piaget gave is that "human knowledge is essentially active. To know is to assimilate reality into systems of transformations. . . . Knowledge, then, is a system of transformations that become progressively adequate" (1970, p. 15). As this statement implies, not all individuals structure their knowledge in precisely the same way, although all individuals may share a common sequence through which knowledge develops. It is this point which places Piaget's epistemology in fundamental contradiction to the epistemology which has informed political scientists' research on belief systems. Both the epistemology and the methods employed in research on belief structure are essentially passive and content-oriented. The concern is with what the individual believes, and no attempt is made to induce the subject to actively construct the relationships among discrete elements of meaning. Furthermore, there are no developmental baselines which can be used to assess the transformational structures of belief organization. In order to move toward the identification of those transformational structures, we must first lay out the ontogeny of intelligence.

The Functional Invariants and Intellectual Development

Piaget focused on the field of intelligence in order to develop genetic epistemology, but it is his peculiar definition of intelligence which accounts for the basic strength of his system. For Piaget, intelligence can only be understood as a biological function: "Intellectual functioning is only a special case, a special extension of biological functioning" (Flavell, 1963, p. 43). As such, intelligence must conform to the basic principles which underlie biological functioning in general: "In Piaget's view, cognitive development must have its roots firmly planted in biological growth, and basic principles valid for the former are to be found only among those which are true of the latter" (Flavell, 1963, p. 36).

The two universal principles of biological functioning are *organization* and *adaptation,* the latter composed of assimilation and accommodation. The whole of Piaget's theory of intelligence, or specifically of cognitive development, can be reduced to these *"functional invariants."* These functions are invariant only in that they are present wherever life is present, from the simplest to the most complex organisms, in every aspect of the organism's functioning. Obviously, the functional invariants vary in terms of the forms they assume, but the function remains the same. Intelligence, then, is defined in terms of organization and adaptation, and the indissociable processes of assimilation and accommodation. Piaget's life work was to trace out the structural vicissitudes to which the functional invariants are subject in the course of intellectual development. It is this work which constitutes the discipline of genetic epistemology.

Since all biological organisms must interact with their environment in order to maintain themselves, Piaget's theory of intelligence is interactionist. The environment interacts with the organism, and the organism interacts with the environment. The two forms of adaptation, assimilation and accommodation, reflect this dynamic interaction: "Adaptation must be described as an equilibrium between the action of the organism on the environment and vice versa. Taking the term in its broadest sense, 'assimilation' may be used to describe the action of the organism on surrounding objects. . . . Conversely, the environment acts on the organism and following the practice of biologists, we can describe this converse action by the term 'accommodation'" (Piaget, 1960, pp. 7–8).

Any form of adaptation presumes an assimilation to, and accommodation of, something.[2] That "something" is organization. In biological functioning the organization is the organism itself; in intellectual functioning organization is represented by intellectual structures: "Intellectual development is an organizational process, and what are organized are active intellectual operations" (Flavell, 1963, p. 168). The various stages in the organization of mental operations represent the structural elements of thought, and the character of these organizational structures depends on the equilibrium between assimilation and accommodation. In Piaget's system the summary term describing this state of equilibrium is the egocentric-sociocentric continuum. It is the key term in developing a structural analysis of political beliefs. Before elaborating upon egocentrism, however, a few more expository points must be made.

The functional invariants are active throughout every stage and period of life, indeed in every action of life. Their function remains the same regardless of the level of development. What changes throughout this process of development are the ways in which the functional invariants are structured. For the question of cognitive development, what characterizes the cognitive structures is the equilibrium between organization and adaptation at the broadest level, and at the level just below this, the equilibrium between accommodation and assimilation. Egocentrism, as we shall see in a moment, is defined in terms of this equilibrium between accommodation and assimilation. The point to note here is that since egocentrism is defined in terms of the functional invariants, and since the functional invariants persist through each stage of development (the stages of development are discussed below), egocentrism itself is subject to the developmental process and manifests itself in different ways in each stage.

If intellectual development is an active process of organizing intellectual operations, what are operations? The building blocks of operations are actions, which form schemas, which in turn are reciprocally coordinated to form operations. Fully developed operations are not achieved until the third period of development, so we must first focus our attention on the building blocks: action-schemas. Sensorimotor intelligence is practical intelligence. It is "aimed at getting results rather than stating truths" (Inhelder and Piaget, 1969, p. 4). This form of intelligence (know-how) obtains results "by constructing a complex system of action schemes" (p. 4). The bases of these action-schemes are our basic behaviors; e.g., sucking, grasping, kicking. The developmental sequence of schemas is as follows: building upon instincts, or genetically determined behavior sequences, we quickly move beyond the specific instinctual messages through repetition, to generalization, and on to differentiation-recognition.

An example should help clarify the sequence. The first attempts by the infant to find the nipple and suck are only randomly successful, but quickly, through repetition, the behavior becomes solidified into a schema (that is, a plan organizing action), and then generalized, as for instance when the infant sucks objects other than the nipple. Gradually the expanded (generalized) range of application becomes differentiated as the environment demands new forms of accommodation for the assimilatory schema: "Repetition consolidates and stabilizes (the single schema) as well as providing the necessary condition for change. Generalization enlarges it by extending its domain of application. And differentiation has the consequence of dividing the originally global schema into new schemas, each with a sharper more discriminating focus on reality" (Flavell, 1963, p. 57).

Each action-schema proceeds through the same series of repetition, generalization, and differentiation, and as development proceeds, single schemas become reciprocally assimilated (coordinated) to form new and expanded action sequences in ever more complex patterns. It should be underlined, for it is fundamental to Piaget's entire conception of intelligence, and it is the factor which sets him apart from other theorists, that intelligence is an *active* process of *construction.* While the environment provides certain restraints upon that activity, it is the organism's activity, generated from within by the organism's needs, which results in intellectual structures.

In the beginning, schemas "are made with the sole support of perception and movements and thus by means of a sensorimotor coordination of actions without the intervention of representation or thought" (Inhelder and Piaget, 1969, p. 4). At the end of the first period the child has achieved physical mastery of the environment, and the entire cycle of development must be repeated on the symbolic level, or the level of representational thought. Indeed, in each succeeding period the child must learn again all of the basic relationships mastered in the preceding period, but from a different perspective on reality. For example, after the sensorimotor period, "there has to be a long and tortuous *redevelopment,* as it were, of space, of causality, of time and all the rest on this new symbolic plane" (Flavell, 1963, p. 149). Development, then, is an expanding spiral. At each succeeding turn in the spiral, development follows the same trajectory but upon a higher, expanding, organizational plane.[3] It must also be stated that the rate of development is not uniform but varies with each basic schema. For example, an individual's grasping the principle of the conservation of mass precedes his or her grasping the principle of the conservation of weight by about two years, yet both operations develop in the same period by means of essentially the same cognitive skills. Each operation has its own ontogenic history, albeit an ontogenic history which is generally isomorphic with the history of other operations.

How, then, can we characterize this ontogenic history of operations? To do so, the reader must have a general handle on the four distinct periods in the development of intellectual structures.

Piaget marked off four major periods describing the equilibrated structures.[4] Each period circumscribes a series of qualitatively different and successively invariant stages. These four periods are as follows: (1) the *sensorimotor* period, from birth to about age two,[5] when language and the capacity for representational thought develop; (2) *preoperational* thought, in which representational thought is consolidated from age two to seven; (3) *concrete operations,* in which the first evidence of complex, tightly integrated systems of actions appears and true operations (characterized by their reversibility) develop, between the ages of seven and eleven; and (4) *formal operations*, in which the capacity for abstract, hypothetico-deductive reasoning is established, between the ages of eleven and fifteen. Each of these four periods can be thought of as different organizations of intelligence, yet each period is built upon and incorporates the achievements of the preceding period(s). The process of development within each period is characterized by a number of important shared characteristics, and as we move on to a delineation of these characteristics we are knocking on the door of egocentrism.

Each of the four different intellectual structures has a different orientation to reality and can be characterized briefly as follows: (1) In the sensorimotor period reality is primarily a perceptual affair based on the action schemas developed through the child's interaction with the environment and vice versa. Intelligence is plain know-how. (2) In the preoperational period action-schemas become internalized and can be internally represented in thought, but this is entirely a staccotic intelligence. That is, reality is a before-the-eye, moment-to-moment reality, a present reality with no history or future. There is a minimum of coordination between schemas and a complete lack of reversibility, such as the ability to move from effect to cause, or from cause to effect, and back again. Reality appears as single-frame rather than continuous-frame: "It is a useful and only slightly misleading generalization about the preoperational child that he has no stable, enduring and internally consistent cognitive organization, no system-in-equilibrium, with which to order, relate, and make coherent, the world around him. His cognitive life, like his affective life, tends to be an unstable, discontinuous, moment-to-moment one" (Flavell, 1963, p. 158). (3) In the concrete operational period the child moves away from "before-the-eye" reality and begins to move from the actual to the potential, but this is only relative to preoperational thought. Concrete operations remain rooted in the actual, and each area of thought is essentially an islet of organization that is unconnected to other islets. To use Flavell's analogy: "The structures of concrete operations are . . . rather like parking lots whose individual parking spaces are now occupied, now empty; the spaces themselves endure, however (as they would not for the pre-operational child), and lead their owner to look beyond the cars actually present towards potential, future occupants of the vacant and vacant-to-be spaces" (1963, p. 203). In short, operations are reversible, cars go in and come out of their spaces. The child will extrapolate from the existing to the potential, but it is a special-case activity. (4) In the period of formal operations reality appears as just one example of all possible realities. The child reverses the concrete orientation from actual to potential and reasons instead from potential to actual, conceiving reality as just a special case of the possible. The adolescent at the level of formal operations possesses a highly integrated, interlocking system, a system by which the child easily moves from one subsystem to another in the course of solving a problem. The essential conditions are, first, that the adolescent *begins* from the extrapolation of the potential *routinely*, and, second, that formal operational thought is characterized by *operations on operations* (which in Piaget's terms are "second-degree operations," scientific operations proper).

We are now in a position to summarize the basic outlines of cognitive development. Simple actions become action-schemas which follow the developmental sequence of repetition, generalization, and differentiation. Schemas then become reciprocally assimilated, and when these schemas begin to show the property of reversibility we can begin to speak of operations. Operations exhibit the following four characteristics:

> First of all, an operation is an action that can be internalized; that is, it can be carried out in thought as well as executed materially. Second, it is a reversible action; that is, it can take place in one direction or in the opposite direction. . . . The third characteristic of an operation is that it always supposes some conversation, some invariant. . . . The fourth characteristic is that no operation exists alone. Every operation is related to a system of operations, or to a total structure as we call it. (Piaget, 1970, pp. 21–22)

Finally, schemas and, later, operations are the basic components of cognitive structures, and these components are organized in four different, successive structures: sensorimotor, preoperational, concrete operational, and formal operational.

Piaget devoted a tremendous effort to tracing these basic operations and their structures, and to go into further detail would take us far beyond what is necessary for our present purposes. The point to be made is that developed *political beliefs are operations*, or in their more primitive form, simply intuitions which exhibit the qualities of preoperational thought. A belief system is composed of countless numbers of these operations joined together in particular, recognizable patterns. The character of these patterns is best described in terms of the degree of egocentrism, the subject to which we now turn.

Egocentrism: The Mainspring
of Genetic Epistemology

The most important concept Piaget has to offer political science as we attempt to develop a structural analysis of belief systems is the concept of egocentrism. Egocentrism was the unifying concept of all of the early seminal studies of reasoning, moral judgment, language, logic, and the concepts of space, movement, causality, and number. Egocentrism plays a role in Piaget's thought similar to the role of libido in Freud's thought, or the role of the labor theory of value in Marx's thought. The analogy can be extended even further: just as Freud's "Project" and Marx's 1844 manuscripts[6] provide basic insights and entrée to their later works, the idea of egocentrism provides the groundwork for entrée to all of Piaget's later writings on cognitive development, even his more developed formulations in which egocentrism per se is not mentioned with any frequency. Even though Piaget gradually moved away from talking in terms of egocentrism in favor of the more precise language of logical algebra and equilibrium theory, egocentrism remains the core of his unparalleled work: "This tendency to substitute mathematical for verbal terminology is not to be taken as a rejection of earlier interpretations in favor of new and different ones. Rather, it is an attempt to discover (or even invent, whenever necessary) mathematical structures which express the essence of these verbally given organizational properties" (Flavell, 1963, p. 181).

In Piaget's later publications (1976, 1978) he returned to verbal, as opposed to mathematical, explications, and although he spoke of egocentrism only once (1978, p. 59) in these studies, it was clear that egocentrism remained the central organizing concept in his vision of how the mind develops. If now the emphasis is upon progress "from the periphery to the center" in the development of conscious conceptualization, it is an emphasis completely consonant with, indeed the very essence of, egocentrism.

It is difficult in a short space to fully delineate the concepts essential to an understanding of Piaget's theory of cognitive development. He used so many different concepts to look at intellectual development that, as Flavell commented, the choice of any one unifier is almost arbitrary. It is arbitrary because first of all the model is holistic, each part interrelated, but also because many of the concepts (e.g., egocentrism, equilibrium, structure, centering, de-centering, states and transformations, transduction, etc.) attack the same problem from different points of view. Piaget considered the various concepts, in Flavell's words, "as multiple expressions of a single cognitive orientation rather than as a string of unconnected attributes" (Flavell, 1963, p. 161). Since Piaget himself preferred the concept of egocentrism as a unifier (1954b, p. 50), and since egocentrism can act as a pivot providing access to the rest of his system, it seems reasonable to continue to use egocentrism to represent that "single cognitive orientation" which Piaget described in so many different ways.

"The concept of intellectual development as a movement from structured disequilibrium to structural equilibrium, repeating itself at ever higher levels of functioning, is a central concept for Piaget" (Flavell, 1963, p. 21). Each stage and each period represents a dynamic equilibrium in a "grand equilibration process." But what is equilibrated? Simply stated, the equilibration is between the organism and the environment on the biological level, between self and other, subject and object, at the psychological, intellectual level. More complexly, the equilibration is between organization and adaptation, which in turn requires an increasingly adequate equilibrium between assimilation and accommodation.

It is the relationship between assimilation and accommodation that is central to the definition of egocentrism. In technical terms, egocentrism can be defined as *a state of mind in which assimilation and accommodation are undifferentiated, yet mutually antagonistic in their functioning.* The most extreme form of egocentrism is total assimilation to self, with minimal accommodation. In less technical terms, egocentrism is the lack of differentiation between self and other:

> The initial state of undifferentiation and antagonism between the functional invariants essentially defines . . . egocentrism. The concept of egocentrism is a most important one in Piaget's thinking and has been from the very earliest writings (e.g., 1926). It denotes a cognitive state in which the cognizer sees the world from a single point of view only—his own—but without knowledge of the existence of (other) viewpoints or perspectives and, a fortiori, without awareness that he is a prisoner of his own. (Flavell, 1963, p. 60)

Piaget described egocentrism in a number of different ways[7] (see the appendix), but perhaps his most succinct description was as follows: "Egocentrism signifies the absence of both self-perception and objectivity" (1954a, p. xiii).

The second fundamental way to define egocentrism is as follows: *the preponderance of perception over conceptualization;* or in more precise Piagetian terms, the *disequilibrium* between perception (an assimilatory activity) and conceptualization (an accommodatory activity). In infantile egocentrism the primacy (or profound disequilibrium) is absolute. In later stages and periods this primacy of perception over conceptualization is relative. Infantile egocentrism is absolute insofar as the objective world must be in direct contact with perceptual activity for the objective world to exist for the infant.

As reality solidifies into predictable relationships, the child becomes aware of himself as an object in a world of objects, and infantile egocentrism passes into personal history. The child's perspective on the physical plane has thus become sociocentric; that is, there is coordination and articulation between self and other, and thus assimilation and accommodation are differentiated and articulated: "Knowledge of self and knowledge of objects are thus the dual resultants of the successive differentiation and equilibration of the invariant functions which characterize sensory-motor development" (Flavell, 1963, p. 62). Thus, with each advance in terms of the articulation and differentiation of accommodation and assimilation, egocentrism is diminished.

Although it would be a simplification, it could be said that egocentrism passes through the same general course of development in each developmental period, but in an attenuated form. Stated differently, each succeeding developmental stage is characterized by a lesser degree of egocentrism relative to the preceding stage, or by a greater degree of egocentrism relative to the stage that follows.[8] What is definitive of egocentrism, then, not only in the sensori-motor period but in all its later manifestations, is the degree of undifferentiation between subject and object, or the preponderance of perception over conceptualization "relative to a differentiation and equilibrium yet to be achieved" (Flavell, 1963, p. 64).

This leads to what is, in terms of the application of egocentrism to the analysis of political beliefs, the most important point to be made in this exposition. Egocentrism appears in successively attenuated form in the beginning of every stage and period of intellectual development. As Flavell pointed out, "Since it is always a subject-object undifferentiation relative to a differentiation and equilibrium yet to be achieved, egocentrism of course reappears in attenuated form at genetic levels beyond those of neonate and preschooler" (1963, p. 65). From stage to stage, period to period, indeed content domain to content domain, development is marked by the gradual attenuation of egocentrism, and this point will have the greatest bearing on the subsequent discussion of egocentrism as it applies to the analysis of the structure of belief systems. The importance of egocentrism is that it is a form of thought which is not limited to childhood or adolescence, but is found in adult thought as well: "In our opinion these beliefs have their interest because the same phenomena reappear in adult mental life and because the psychological facts lead by a series of intermediate steps to metaphysical systems themselves" (Piaget, 1965, p. 75).

Before moving on to the conditions which foster or inhibit egocentrism, there is another way of defining egocentrism which must be explicated. Directly related to the disequilibrium between assimilation and accommodation, and the primacy of perception over conceptualization, a third way of formulating the concept of egocentrism is as follows: Egocentrism begins by focusing on the periphery and only gradually moves to the center. In the egocentric perspective attention is focused upon the immediately perceptible, observable factors, to the neglect of the internal regulations which produce what is immediately observable. In short, there is attention to effect, without concern for cause, a focus on the surface, to the neglect of the underlying processes.

To recapitulate, there are three main ways to define egocentrism (supplemented by the statements in the appendix): (1) egocentrism consists of the disequilibrium between assimilation and accommodation; (2) egocentrism is the preponderance of perception over conceptualization; and (3) egocentrism describes the state of cognizance which focuses on the periphery and gradually moves in the direction of the center regions of actions and regulations.

In each developmental manifestation of egocentrism, the goal of development[9] is a more adequate grasp of reality leading to achievement of the sociocentric perspective, in which there is articulation and coordination between the functional invariants and between self and the environment: "We have seen how these successive constructions always involve a decentering of the initial egocentric point of view in order to place it in an ever-broader coordination of relations and concepts, so that each new terminal grouping further integrates the subject's activity by adapting it to an ever widening reality" (Piaget, 1967, p. 69).

One consequence of the "ever-broader coordination of relations and concepts" is an expanded capacity for role-taking activity,[10] a consequence which bears directly upon the question of ideology. As the individual engages in multiple relations, he or she can construct more adequate models of social causality through the ability to place the self in the position of another and so to see the world from the other's point of view. The egocentric thinker sees only one point of view—his or her own—while the sociocentric thinker is able to entertain various possible perspectives and to judge how specific actions will affect different perspectives. In short, the egocentric perspective is unidimensional, the sociocentric multidimensional. The sociocentric perspective permits more flexible responses to political problems, as well as an expanded capacity to direct political action effectively. Corresponding to this greater flexibility is the decline of dogmatism as one moves closer to the sociocentric point of view. Empirically, it should be the case that egocentrism and dogmatism are close associates, affiliated by their common unidimensional perspective.[11]

The relationship of egocentrism to the functional invariants has been explicated and its place in the development of intellectual structures located, but little has been said concerning the basic qualities by which egocentric thought can be identified and understood. In order to apply egocentrism in belief systems analysis, we shall briefly characterize egocentrism as it is found in each of the four major periods of cognitive development.

1. *Infantile egocentrism* is characterized primarily by the lack of object permanence. Lack of object permanence results from the assimilation of reality to the self *solely* on the basis of the infant's own immediate sensorimotor activity. Assimilation is in utter preponderance over accommodation, which is at its least progressed state. Reality is discontinuous and dependent upon immediate perception: "In effect, for the newborn child there is no space that contains objects, since there are no objects (including the body proper which naturally is not conceived of as an object). There is a series of spaces differing one from another and all centered on the body proper . . . but they lack coordination with each other. Thus there are egocentric spaces, we might say, not coordinated and not including the body itself as an element in a container" (Piaget, 1973, p. 15).

It is the construction of a concept of the permanent object which leads to the coordination of the various discontinuous sensual spaces into universal space containing both self and other/object: "The initial absence of substantive objects, followed by the construction of solid and permanent objects, is the first example of the transition from primitive, total egocentricity to the final elaboration of an external universe" (Piaget, 1967, reprint of 1940 article, p. 14). As the world becomes substantiated, there is a parallel development on the physical plane of the child's sense of causality, which is based on the child's own motor activity, along with a sense of time which is based on a sense of speed (speed, it turns out, is a primitive intuition, while time is an intellectual construction). The goal of development in this sensorimotor period, then, is an awareness of an objective self and an objective environment.

2. *Preoperatory, or intuitive, egocentrism* is best understood as a recapitulation of infantile egocentrism on the level of symbolic, or, better, representational thought. That is, there is the same lack of differentiation between self and other. This lack of differentiation is best understood in terms of the child's inability to place the self in the position of another, simply because the other's point of view is understood (assimilated) only from the child's own perspective: "Piaget uses [egocentrism] to mean the child's inability to take another's point of view. It is not a pejorative term with respect to the child since the child does not take another's point of view because he *cannot* as opposed to the egocentric adult who can take another's point of view but will not" (Elkind, in the introduction to Piaget, 1967). The experimental evidence of this inability is quite extensive.[12] A concrete example is the young child's inability to distinguish right from left from another's point of view. For example, as early as age two and a half, some children can distinguish the right and left parts of their own bodies, and when sitting next to another person can distinguish the right and left parts of the other's body. But if facing the other person, the child simply "mirrors" his body onto the other such that the other's right arm is designated as the left arm.

Piaget has many documented examples of this kind of failure to transpose spatial relations (see, in particular, Piaget and Inhelder, 1956). A typical experiment to test the child's ability to place himself in the position of another was as follows. When a doll is moved around a pasteboard model of three differently colored mountains, and the child is shown snapshots of ten different perspectives on the model, the preoperative child cannot correctly select which perspective is that of the doll. In fact, each change in perspective remains undifferentiated: the child continues to pick his own perspective as that of the doll's or a random perspective, "indicating that, so far as the child is concerned, all the pictures are equally suitable for all points of view" (Piaget and Inhelder, 1956, p. 213). In short, all points of view are assimilated to the child's own individual point of view:

> However dependent he may be on surrounding intellectual influences, the young child assimilates them in his own way. He reduces them to his point of view and therefore distorts them without realizing it, simply because he can not yet distinguish his point of view from that of others through failure to coordinate or "group" the points of view. Thus, both on the social and on the physical plane, he is egocentric through ignorance of his own subjectivity. . . . Intellectual egocentricity is . . . nothing more than a lack of coordination, a failure to "group" relations with other individuals as well as with other objects. (Piaget, 1960, pp. 160–161)

The consequences of this inability to take the point of view of another are of fundamental importance in defining the overall quality of preoperatory, or intuitive, thought. Further, the consequences of this inability can be seen to operate in adults whose political beliefs are structured on an order comparable to the intuitive thought of the child: "One quality stands out in the thinking of the young child: he constantly makes assertions without trying to support them with facts. This lack of attempts at proof stems from the character of the child's social behavior . . . from his egocentricity conceived as a lack of differentiation between his own point of view and that of others. It is only vis-à-vis others that we are led to seek evidence for our statements" (Piaget, 1967, p. 29). Further: "Far from helping the subject distinguish between his and other viewpoints, the egocentric attitude tends to encourage him to accept it without question as the only one possible" (Piaget and Inhelder, 1956, p. 194).[13]

3. *The egocentrism of concrete operational thought* is best conceived of as the taking of existing reality as the only possible reality. The distinctions here become more difficult and more technical,

particularly as the child enters the later stages of concrete operations in which a fairly adequate logic is operative. In its final stages
concrete thought is logical and capable of reversibility, but it is tied
directly to concrete existing reality, and that reality remains fairly
compartmentalized; that is, reality is a set of subsystems which
have not been reciprocally assimilated into a single overall integrated system of possible realities. The child is capable of forming
groupings and groups, but the use of lattice structures remains relatively undeveloped insofar as lattice structures entail *all possible*
relations among a set of elements rather than simply the existing
relations.

In order to describe concrete thought, we must contrast it with
the fourth period, formal thought. The essential differences between
concrete and formal operations are two: formal operations are operations on operations (second-order operations) and are characterized
by being a combinatorial system (see Piaget and Inhelder, 1969, p.
113). It is important to note that the logical operations in the early
stages of the concrete period are still tied to the subject's own actions. Later, when concrete logic is completed and formal operations
begin, the adolescent will be able to perform the same operations
from a hypothetical position without the aid of a concrete "experiment." The adolescent will understand the underlying principles
rather than simply the overt relationships.

The course of development in the concrete period is to banish
egocentric perception in favor of concrete operations: "It is operations that result in a correction of perceptual intuition—which is
always a victim of illusions of the moment—and which 'decenter'
egocentricity so as to transform transitory relationships into a coherent system of objective, permanent relations" (Piaget, 1967,
p. 46).

A clear example of the egocentrism of the concrete period is in the
realm of moral reasoning, a field which already has been shown to
be of particular political relevance.[14] Piaget identified three basic
stages in the consciousness of rules. The first is the "egocentric"
stage (roughly, although not completely, isometric with the preoperatory period) when rules are not coercive. Adherence to rules is
a matter of little consequence; each child either has a special set of

rules of his own, or received rules are seen simply as interesting examples rather than obligatory realities. During the second stage (which is roughly equivalent to the period of concrete operations) "rules are regarded as sacred and untouchable, emanating from adults and lasting forever. Every suggested alteration strikes the child as a transgression" (Piaget, 1965, p, 28). (This stage corresponds to Kohlberg's stages three and four, the "Good Boy" and "Law and Order" orientations.) During the third stage (roughly corresponding to the onset of formal operations) "a rule is looked upon as a law due to mutual consent, which you must respect if you want to be logical but which is permissible to alter on the condition of enlisting general opinion on your side" (p. 28). Concrete egocentrism, then, is the perception of existing reality as the only possible reality. Rules are literally as inflexible as concrete. In this case there is the same disequilibrium between assimilation and accommodation, and between perception and conceptualization; i.e., perceived rules are the only possible rules conceivable. There is also a lack of reversibility in the sense that rules cannot be changed or undone. A transitory position between concrete rules and rules based on mutual consent is the position that a rule can change but it is not a "true" rule even if everyone agrees to it.

The major difference between concrete and formal orientations toward rules is that the former takes into account only the surface compliance, not the underlying principle of the rule or the intent of the rule violator (e.g., in primitive law there is often no accommodation for accidental homicide; homicide is homicide). In contrast, formal operatory orientations toward rules take into account the rule's purpose (the principles or propositions) as well as the individual's intent. In short, there is a concept of justice which recognizes the spirit and not simply the letter of the law; there is a sense of justice which recognizes the possibility of conflicting laws, pressures, and special circumstances; there is a sense of justice which does not center on the rule itself, but decenters the perspective to include the context in which the rule comes into play.

4. *The adolescent egocentrism of formal operational thought,* as treated by Piaget, is not entirely satisfactory. Piaget's treatment of adolescent egocentrism is too content-oriented, and as a result, as

more research is conducted, the concept will undergo reformulation. With that caution in mind, we turn to a brief description of adolescent egocentrism.

Adolescent egocentrism is the result of the burgeoning capacity of formal thought to encompass multiple versions of reality. It is, in effect, a second "Copernican revolution" (the first is in the sensorimotor period), in which reality becomes simply one rather mundane and imperfect example of all possible realities. Adolescent egocentrism is the distortion of thought assimilated to itself without adequate accommodation of reality:

> In accordance with a law we have already seen manifested in the infant and the child, each new mental ability starts off by incorporating the world in a process of egocentric assimilation. Only later does it attain equilibrium through a compensating accommodation to reality. The intellectual egocentricity of adolescence is comparable to the egocentricity of the infant who assimilates the universe into his own corporal activity and that of the young child who assimilates things into his own nascent thought (symbolic play, etc.). Adolescent egocentricity is manifested by belief in the omnipotence of reflection, as though the world should submit itself to idealistic schemes rather than to systems of reality. It is the metaphysical age *par excellence*: the self is strong enough to reconstruct the universe and big enough to incorporate it. . . . The metaphysical egocentricity of the adolescent is gradually lessened as a reconciliation between formal thought and reality is effected. Equilibrium is attained when the adolescent understands that the proper function of reflection is not to contradict but to predict and interpret experience. (Piaget, 1967, p. 64)

Since there are in fact situations in which it is necessary to contradict experience and to refuse to accept reality as it presents itself, too close an adherence to Piaget's description can mislead. The essential point, however, is that the adolescent operates with a certain dogmatism and an incessant jamming of reality into his own formal categories and relations. There is a certain closed-mindedness and failure to accommodate thought to reality. But once thought accommodates reality, the individual is capable of truly transforming reality (at least on the plane of social relations) through the ability to interpret and predict experience. The manner in which the individual arrives at this position is the subject of the next section.

Cooperation: The Scourge of Egocentrism

The direct and fundamental relationship between egocentrism and cooperation goes to the core of social life and has the most far-reaching implications for the organization of society and the development of individual ideas. To begin with, if we dissect the word into "co" and "operation," we get an initial insight into the special importance of cooperation for Piaget. Cooperation is a joint operation. Any form of cooperation implies a coordination of viewpoints, of ends and means, and it requires, therefore, a sociocentric, as opposed to an egocentric, perspective. This section examines the role that cooperation plays in the transition from egocentric to sociocentric thinking.

Piaget's most extensive formulation of the role of cooperation in the development of mental structures is in *The Moral Judgment of the Child* (1965), although he returns to the issue in a number of other studies, e.g., chapter six of *The Psychology of Intelligence* (1960), and the first essay of *Six Psychological Studies* (1967). The treatment of cooperation in the book on moral judgment is directly related to the findings of four other studies which, along with that book, form the five early classics of Piaget's career. *The Moral Judgment of the Child* is a sort of capstone to the work on language (1926), reasoning (1928), reality (1929), and causality (1930), and like all capstones it must bear a direct relation to the elements to which it is joined while still playing a slightly different functional role.

In this case the direct relation with the previous studies was the identification of the moral realism which parallels the intellectual realism of the young child as well as the further development of the idea of egocentrism. The slightly different function was to turn the focus of attention from the strictly psychological mechanisms to the related mechanisms of socialization. In this work, more than in the others, Piaget is particularly concerned with pedagogical and sociological questions bearing upon the manner in which the child is socialized. Hence, *The Moral Judgment of the Child* is probably the most directly relevant of Piaget's books for political scientists. Its relevance to politics lies in the fact that its central focus is the relationship between authority and cooperation, which, of course, is of profound importance in the political world. In addition, much of political philosophy is concerned with judgments of "The Good" (not to mention the central role of moral reasoning for individual political judgments), and paying attention to the manner in which our tools of judgment are shaped can only aid us in their employment: "In a sense, child morality throws light on adult morality. If we want to form men and women, nothing will fit us so well for the task as to study the laws that govern their formation" (*Moral Judgment*, p. 9). So what are those "laws of formation"?

The core issue explored in *Moral Judgment* is the collaboration of authority (constraint), egocentrism, and moral realism on one hand, and the collaboration of cooperation, operatory thought, and moral autonomy on the other. Throughout Piaget's exposition, authority is opposed to cooperation, or, more precisely, cooperation is conceived of as the "ideal equilibrium toward which all relations of constraint tend" (1965, p. 90). The basic theme (or law of formation) is that constraint reinforces the child's initial egocentric perspective and maintains moral realism, while cooperation weakens egocentrism and fosters moral autonomy. In short, there are two moralities, derived from two distinct forms of social relations: a morality of constraint, or of heteronomy, and a morality of cooperation, or of autonomy.

These two types of morality, deriving from two types of social relations, are not limited to childhood socialization:

> Social constraint—and by this we mean any social *relation into which there enters the element of authority* and which is not, like cooperation, the result of an interchange between equal individuals—has on the individual results that are analogous to those exercised by adult constraint on the mind of the child.

> *The two phenomena, moreover, are really one and the same thing,* and the adult who is under the dominion of unilateral respect for the "Elders" and for tradition is really behaving like a child. (Piaget, 1965, p. 340; emphasis added)

The implications for social structure are obvious and overwhelming. Social infantilization produces a psychology of dependence in which unilateral respect for authority is among the most prominent characteristics.

As long as an element of authority exists in the interaction between individuals, there is, by definition, an imbalance in their social relations. That is, the authority of one negates the authority of the other(s), and we cannot speak of "co-" operation, or mutual actions, but of a unilateral determination of action. Naturally, "pure" cooperation and "pure" constraint are rare, if not impossible, in actual human relations, but they can be thought of as the limiting "ideals" between which all forms of human interaction fall. This becomes clearer if we think of cooperation in terms of reciprocity, and reciprocity as the social equivalent of logical reversibility (the essential requirement for operatory thought). Reciprocity is based on mutual, as opposed to unilateral, respect. The egocentric child cannot cooperate because of the lack of reciprocity represented by the failure to differentiate his own point of view from that of others:

> So long as the child does not dissociate his ego from the suggestions coming from the social world, he cannot cooperate, for in order to cooperate, one must be conscious of one's ego and situate it in relation to thought in general. And in order to become conscious of one's ego it is necessary to liberate oneself from the thought and will of others. The coercion exercised by the adult or the older child is therefore inseparable from the unconscious egocentricity of the very young child. (Piaget, 1965, p. 93)

With mutual respect there is a complete reversibility between equals, and action is dependent upon mutual agreement rather than command; and this is the key to the special role cooperation plays in the development of moral autonomy and operatory thought. To reach agreement—that is, to coordinate viewpoints—requires an exchange of ideas, a differentiation of viewpoints and their integration. It means that individuals must have a shared system of meaning which requires a consistency of meaning and a certain "morality" in their thought: "Logic is the morality of thought, just as morality is the logic of action" (Piaget, 1965, p. 398). Shared logical structures permit cooperation:

> The obligation not to contradict oneself is not simply a conditional necessity for anybody who accepts the exigencies of operational activity; it is also a moral "categorical" imperative, inasmuch as it is indispensable for intellectual interaction and cooperation. And, indeed, the child first seeks to avoid contradicting himself when it is in the presence of others. In the same way, objectivity, the need for verification, the need for words and ideas to keep their meaning constant, etc., are as much social obligations as conditions of operational thought. (Piaget, 1960, p. 163)

Cooperation, then, forces upon the child an awareness of the need to justify his own point of view, to substantiate his perspective, so that the child becomes aware simultaneously of both his own point of view and that of the other(s). For this reason the onset of true cooperation between children and the onset of operatory thought are contemporaneous developments:

> The more intuitions articulate themselves and end by grouping themselves operationally, the more adept the child becomes at cooperation, a social relationship which is quite distinct from coercion in that it involves a reciprocity between individuals who know how to differentiate their viewpoints. As far as intelligence is concerned, cooperation is thus an objectively conducted discussion (out of which arises internalized discussion, i.e., deliberation or reflection), collaboration in work, exchange of ideas, mutual control (the origin of the need for verification

and demonstration), etc. It is therefore clear that cooperation is the first of a series of forms of behavior which are important for the construction and development of logic. (Piaget, 1960, p. 162)

Thus, "at about the age of seven the child becomes capable of cooperation because he no longer confuses his own point of view with that of others. He is able to dissociate his point of view from that of others and to coordinate these different points of view" (Piaget, 1967, p. 39). Cooperation, then, counters intuitive thought—thought, that is, characterized by transduction, phenomenalism, animism, finalism, artificialism, or, in short, egocentricity—and brings the child onto the plane of objective relationships. "It is discussion and mutual criticism that urge us to analyze things; left to ourselves, we are quickly satisfied with a 'global,' and consequently, a subjective explanation" (Piaget, 1965, p. 194).

A Summary of the Piagetian System

Although it is a nearly impossible task, we attempt in the following few pages to summarize Piaget's general perspective on cognitive structures.

The life of the mind is one with the life of the organism. Both the organism's behavior and environmental exigencies, bonded together, contribute to the development of intellectual structures. These intellectual structures are adaptations produced by the biological functions of assimilation and accommodation. Assimilation is the action of the organism on the environment, and accommodation is the action of the environment on the organism. These processes are common to all forms of biological functioning, including psychological functioning. The functions are invariant, while the structures produced by these processes take on various forms.

The overall tendency of biological functioning, and hence of psychological functioning, is toward equilibrium. The various intellectual structures are simply empirically identifiable points of equilibrium between assimilation and accommodation. The functional invariants operate according to the laws of equilibrium and transformation (see Piaget, 1977) as do the structures created by the functional invariants.

All forms of intellectual activity are built upon the organism's activity in interaction with the environment. Intelligence is neither a reflection of the environment nor a vital expression of the organism itself, but a product of the organism and the environment operating in conjunction.

Intellectual structures are built up from instinctive, hereditary reflex actions, and on through the first motor habits, which become, in turn, schemas, operations, and operations on operations. These actions are organized into four successive, invariant periods, each with a succession of different structures representing an ever more precise adaptational equilibrium with the environment. The four periods are designated in the following order: sensorimotor, preoperational, concrete operational, and formal operational thought.

Development within each stage and period is rhythmic and cyclical, both on the plane of behavior and on the plane of consciousness (which is ruled by the "law of conscious realization": consciousness lags behind activity). This development is marked by both horizontal and vertical decalage, meaning development repeats itself on each new plane of activity or consciousness (vertical decalage) and within each plane development repeats itself (horizontal decalage) in each new domain of activity (remembering that thought itself is activity, albeit internalized and abstract in its most developed stages). This rhythmic, cyclical development is characterized by movement from the egocentric perspective to a de-centered, sociocentric perspective. It is through the demands of cooperation, the mutual regulation of operations, that the individual moves out of the egocentric perspective. Thus, cooperation is the most effective means of socialization.

All forms of behavior (which for Piaget refers to "all action directed by the organism toward the outside world in order to change conditions therein or to change their own situation in relation to these surroundings" [Piaget, 1978, p. ix]) entail two inseparable components and corresponding structures: the affective component, which produces the motivating energy for all behavior and can be reduced, following Claparede, to *need*, which is always an expression of disequilibrium (Piaget, 1967, p. 6); and the cognitive component, which structures behavior designed to satisfy the affective need. There is a constant parallel between affective and cognitive life, the structure of one affecting the structure of the other.

Finally, the patterns of thought found in childhood recur in adult life. Intellectual development is not a once-and-for-all affair. In each new area that we confront, each fresh contact with the environment, the construction of our ideas begins by first assimilating what is offered to our own egocentric perspective (egocentric in the sense that we have not yet accommodated the old to the new). Only later is a new, more equilibrated perspective constructed. While the process may be more accelerated in adult life than in childhood, the process continues to parallel the cycles of previous adaptation.

Reprise

As our explication of Piaget's system should make clear, since development is uneven, both within the individual and in comparison with others, different individuals may reason in fundamentally different ways. The observer cannot assume that if two individuals share a set of specific beliefs those beliefs are structured in the same way. Consequently, the Lockean assumption that all individuals reason in fundamentally the same way is an unreliable assumption on which to base the analysis of the structure of belief systems. Likewise, the research which has been guided by this assumption must be called into question. The assumption that a singular pattern of reasoning structures all thought guarantees that no alternative structures will be discovered. In essence, the discipline itself suffers from egocentrism. We have focused on the surface content, to the neglect of the underlying regulating structures of thought.

Moving out of the "what-goes-with-what" paradigm will be difficult. Aside from the fact that careers and whole bodies of literature have been built up around the class inclusion concept of structure, the greatest difficulties will arise as a result of the methodological consequences for research design deriving from a shift to the Kantian/Piagetian perspective. First, we cannot assume that beliefs have meaning unto themselves. Consequently, we cannot explore belief systems by considering subjects' responses to short survey items. Instead, we must ask subjects to actively generate the meaning attached to discrete elements of belief. This will involve a great deal more time devoted to interviews, as well as more time devoted to the analysis of the interviews. Surveys will still be useful, but only as a starting point. Attached to each item designed to elicit *what* a subject believes, we will have to attach a series of questions asking the subject to explain *why* he or she holds a particular belief. The purpose of these questions will not be to understand casual factors behind particular beliefs, but to provide opportunities for the subject to reveal the structure of reasoning producing those beliefs.

Correlational analysis of specific belief items will be of little value. We will have to rely instead on more qualitative judgments, organized by coding categories such as those used in the analysis of group dynamics (Mann, 1967), cognitive mapping (George, 1969), or content analysis (Eldridge, 1983). The attention, of course, will be on the underlying logic of relations, and therefore we will have to employ methodologies associated with formal logical analysis. In short, only by exploring *how* elements of meaning are joined can we identify the underlying cognitive structure. Catalogs of issue positions can identify only the content of cognitive structures, not the structures themselves. The next three chapters illustrate this point by applying Piaget's genetic epistemology to the analysis of both individual belief systems and the development of political culture.

The Structure of the Idea of Democracy in Eastport

If politics can be described as the struggle over the definition of reality, then one of the bloodier battles has been the struggle over the definition of democracy. Both as a concept and as a form of government, democracy has suffered almost every form of degradation and exaltation. Governments as disparate as those of fifth-century Athens, Weimar Germany, the present regime in Afghanistan, and modern New England town meetings have all laid claim to the democratic label. Not to be undone by mere politicians, political scientists have produced an equally bewildering array of conceptual varieties of democracy, including unitary, adversarial, consociational, empirical, normative, polyarchical, direct, and representative versions (among others; see Dahl, 1956; Lijphart, 1977; Mansbridge, 1980; and Pennock, 1979). At the risk of adding to the confusion, two further conceptual varieties are proposed: egocentric and sociocentric democracy. In this chapter the cognitive structure underlying the idea of democracy is explored in a most unrepresentative sample of common citizens.

The subjects of this study are adult children of the fifteen men interviewed in 1958 by Robert E. Lane for his book, *Political Ideology* (1962). The men Lane interviewed all lived in a government-subsidized low-income housing project designed to serve the needs of stable working-class families. To qualify for admission to the project, the subjects had to show incomes falling within strict upper and lower limits; and, most importantly, the household head had to have a stable work record during the two years preceding admission to the program. Lane randomly selected the men from the list of registered voters (women and blacks were excluded), producing a group from various ethnic, religious, and occupational backgrounds. The group included Catholics, Protestants, and Jews, and men from Irish, Polish, Italian, German, and English origins. The occupations pursued were mostly within the working class, including tradesmen, salesmen, clerks, policemen, a bookkeeper, and one graduate student at a local university.

Lane's book became a classic in political science literature and played a major role in the debate over the structure of beliefs in mass publics. For the most part Lane focused on the affective dimensions of belief structure, arguing that personality and unique life experiences gave each man a particular view of the world. That view might not follow a strict political logic, but a clear psychological structure could be discerned. In 1976, in an attempt to add cognitive and intergenerational dimensions to Lane's study, Ward returned to "Eastport" and interviewed the two oldest children of the men in Lane's sample.[1]

The thirty children were divided equally between males and females, ranging in age from eighteen to forty-two. While the age spread appears considerable, the two extremes were single outliers. Two-thirds of the thirty children were within two years of the median age of twenty-seven. For the most part there was little intergenerational social mobility. The bookkeeper's daughters were legal and medical secretaries, the policeman's sons were policemen, the tradesmen's sons were tradesmen, and so forth. There was also little geographical mobility. Three-quarters of the subjects lived within a twenty-mile radius of Eastport.

The data upon which this chapter is based, then, were part of a much larger project which explored the role of generational relations in the development of political beliefs.[2] Among the issues explored in the full project were conceptual differences in the idea of democracy between the two generations. Important intergenerational, as well as intragenerational, differences were found in the structure of the idea of democracy. In this chapter the focus is primarily on the intragenerational differences.

The material was collected over the course of six- to ten-hour interviews with each subject. The interviews replicated Lane's original questions with the addition of current political topics and, most important, questions designed to assess the cognitive structure of the subjects' belief systems. To that end the interviews were open-ended and wide-ranging. The structure of the interview was such that questions went from the abstract to the concrete in each area of concern. For example, sections on democracy, freedom, equality, government, political parties, nationality, and the like all began by asking a question on the order of "What is your understanding of the term . . ." democracy, freedom, and so forth. Then in each area the questions became more and more specific, focusing, for example, on specific leaders rather than "leaders and people." In addition, specific questions designed to draw out the structure of thought were attached to each section. The central questions here asked subjects to negate the concept in question (e.g., "What would you consider to be undemocratic?") or to adjust their personal perspectives by putting themselves in the place of a political leader or racial minority, or in a different political context (e.g., "What would your life have been like if you had been black," or ". . . if you had grown up in the Third World?"). The main question, however, was simply "Why do you believe that?" asked repeatedly, producing a chain of justifications revealing the subject's reasoning about particular issues. It is to that chain of justifications that the remainder of the chapter is devoted.

Of Supermarkets, National Parks, and Other Democratic Wonders

Literally, "democracy" means government by the people.[3] The word refers to a system of government in which ultimate authority is vested in the people. As such, democracy is a procedure for the exercise of power; it is a form of decision making. Democracy, then, is a political term. It does not refer to any particular economic sys-

tem nor any specific form of social relations. Of course, the word
can be brought to bear on economic and social relations, but only
insofar as it describes the form of decision making by which power
within each sphere is allocated and exercised by the constituent
people. Naturally, economic and social interactions are related to
political arrangements, in whatever form those arrangements appear, but there is no intrinsic form of economic or social structure
that flows inexorably from democratic government; after all, in a
democracy the people can come to any economic or social decisions
they choose. Not even majority rule is definitive of democracy, for
self-government can be achieved through consensual processes as
well. Majority rule is simply one decision-rule by which democracy
can be achieved. What is intrinsic to democracy is that decisions
must be sanctioned by the consent of the governed. How that consent is obtained is an altogether different question with several possible answers.

We emphasize the point because it is one easily lost in popular
concepts of democracy. Indeed, among the thirty Eastportians interviewed, the majority made no reference whatsoever to procedural
democracy in their discussion of democracy. Surely, democracy is
more than procedure. It has an intimate relationship to other concepts such as equality, freedom, community, citizenship, friendship, and so forth. But for the majority of the Eastportians, democracy and freedom were essentially undifferentiated, the terms used
interchangeably. When pressed to elaborate, fairly complex ideas of
freedom might be employed, but not a word about consent of the
governed, majority rule, minority rights, or representation was expressed. For example, asked "What is your understanding of democracy?", responses included:

> "You mean freedom? . . . I don't really know what democratic
> means. What does that mean? I would just say Democrat or
> Republican."

> "I don't know. I really can't point to exactly what democracy
> means. That we live in a democracy, or, I don't know. What
> exactly does it mean? I really don't know. I feel so stupid. Peo-

ple come around and say 'Oh, you live in a democracy,' I don't know exactly what they are talking about when they say that."

"I really don't know to tell you the truth. I really don't know. I'm ashamed, but I don't know."

"A way of life, I guess."

"Democracy to me is just trying to be fair and trying to look at it from all angles, and trying to, uh, try to solve the most important problems and just go down the list."

"Freedom of choice in anything you want to do, short of killing somebody or kidnapping or stuff like that. . . . Uh, I think just the general freedom, the use of our natural resources, our parks and camping sites. Uh, the protection we have."

The fact that there is a relationship between concepts by no means implies that the joined concepts are identical. Yes, democracy without freedom is inconceivable and democracy may well be the best guarantee of freedom, but nevertheless democracy and freedom are two different concepts. The question is, is there any structural reason why these two concepts should be confounded?

The argument to be made is that the reason these Eastportians do not differentiate democracy and freedom is that egocentric structuring processes underlie the manifestation of this particular content. As developed in chapter three, egocentrism can be formally defined in three separate, but similar, ways: (1) egocentrism consists of the disequilibrium between assimilation and accommodation; (2) egocentrism is the preponderance of perception over conceptualization; and (3) egocentrism describes the state of cognizance which focuses on the periphery and gradually moves in the direction of the center regions of actions and regulations. In this chapter the formal definitions of egocentrism have been operationalized along four different lines. Each of the four areas is separate, but only taken together do they discriminate between egocentric and sociocentric concepts of democracy. No one criterion is sufficient to identify egocentrism. Of the four basic criteria which will be used to identify egocentric concepts of democracy, two are based on logical operations, one on environmental/behavioral factors, and one on content. Although the discussion begins with the content-based measure, the reader should not conclude that the content measure is of primary importance. The reason for beginning with content is to illustrate how a different theory leads to quite different inferences about how people manipulate political concepts and information, and why it is necessary to go beyond content to cognitive operations and environmental factors in order to verify inferences made from content.

The content-based criterion for identifying egocentric concepts of democracy stems from the confounding of democracy and freedom. Indeed, it is this lack of differentiation (itself a cognitive operation) which is an identifying mark of egocentric concepts of democracy. (In socialist countries, the content-based criterion might well be the lack of differentiation between democratic principles and principles of social equality.) Concomitant with the confounding of democracy and freedom, egocentric concepts of democracy are completely void of any principles commonly associated with the practice of democracy. In place of consent of the governed, majority rule, minority rights, equal political rights, representation, and the like are descriptions of everyday life in America. In Eastport daily activities—comings and goings, making and spending money, vacations, and access to nature provided by national parks—were the focus of attention among those with egocentric concepts of democracy.

This focus points to the three definitions of egocentrism outlined in chapter three. The egocentric thinker produces a concept of democracy by assimilating everyday life in America to the elementary knowledge that America is a democracy. Everyday life is simply recapitulated without accommodating the assimilated material to any principles derived from the actual practice of democracy in the environment (definition 1). That is, the perception of everyday life outweighs any conceptualization of democracy (definition 2). The focus of attention is on the effects of our social and political system. There is no coordination between the products of democracy and the process of democracy (definition 3). The internal mechanisms, the operations and regulations producing a democratic society and polity, are ignored in favor of the periphery, the surface products of democracy. Thus, from the content of the Eastportians' discussion of democracy, one can infer the influence of the structuring processes which are our operationalized definitions of egocentrism.

Still, this is not much different from the traditional content-based ideological measures commonly used by political scientists. It is simply that a different theory is relied upon to make the inferences. To move beyond content-based measures entails asking respondents questions that require them to manipulate the logic of democratic principles. (Again, the order in which the criteria are discussed does not imply that one criterion is more important than another. Since we are dealing with structural components which are interrelated, the discussion just as easily could have begun with cognitive operations and moved on to content.) The two criteria based on logical operations that identify egocentric cognitive structures are the inability to negate the idea of democracy, and the use of inductive, rather than deductive, logic in discussing concrete applications of democratic principles.

In Eastport the watershed between those with an operatory, sociocentric concept of democracy and those with a concrete, egocentric concept of democracy was the question, "What would you consider to be undemocratic?" Ralph DeAngelo provides a response typical of those with egocentric concepts of democracy: "My mind is blank on that"; likewise, Alice Sokolsky responded: "I really can't think of anything that is undemocratic. They should investigate the way people are living."

Those with a concrete, egocentric grasp of democracy were unable to respond to the undemocratic question because they do not have any firm idea of the principles of democracy. We know from the work of Wason and Johnson-Laird (1972) that negation requires an additional step in the reasoning process. Piaget made a similar point: "In brief, everything is aimed at the primacy of the positive during the elementary stages, and the positive corresponds to what, on the level of experience, represents the 'immediate data', whereas negation depends either on derived verifications or on more or less labored constructions as determined by the complexity of the systems" (Piaget, 1977, p. 17). To negate, one must first affirm, but this is precisely what the Eastportians with egocentric concepts of democracy were unable to do.

The second distinguishing criterion based on logical operations is the tendency to reason inductively rather than deductively. There were some among the Eastportians who confused democracy and freedom and were unable to negate the concept and *were* able to reason from specific experiences to abstract democratic principles. They were unable, however, to deduce democratic practices from democratic principles. In short, they could reason from part to whole, but not from whole to part. Logical operations lacked the quality of reversibility which Piaget identified as the distinguishing difference between sociocentric and egocentric logic. For example, Jeff Johnson, a construction worker, described the selection of union officers as follows: "It's a farce. They ask for nominations from the floor. You can only nominate the people in office. The nominators are preselected. All it needs is one vote. The recording secretary casts the vote. . . . If you disagree with what is being said you end up with a beating, if not physically, they find a way to get you off the job. Any big union is the same. They are run by a select few." Here is a clear criticism of his union for its undemocratic practices, yet five minutes before Jeff made no mention of such basic principles in his discussion of democracy in general. The democratic ideas are there, but they are embedded in concrete structures. That is, they can be applied to familiar and specific examples, from the particular to the general, but not from the general to the particular. Mature cognitive operations are reversible, and it is precisely the lack of reversibility which we see in Jeff Johnson's treatment of democracy.

Not all of those exhibiting the other aspects of egocentrism were able to reason inductively about democracy. In contrast, all those who confused democracy and freedom had trouble negating the concept of democracy, an operation which requires reversibility. Since some were able to apply principles in concrete situations, we may be dealing with subjects at different levels of egocentrism. This suggests that a series of intermediate concepts may lie embedded in the single overarching category described herein. Thus, further research with larger subject pools will be necessary to identify the intermediate stages in the structural development of the idea of democracy.

The environmental/behavioral criterion distinguishing egocentric from sociocentric concepts of democracy is a question of exposure to democratic processes and opportunities to engage in democratic practice. A fundamental axiom of Piaget's theory of cognitive development is that consciousness follows on the heels of action. There comes a time when consciousness can direct action, but in the early stages behavior precedes consciousness. One would expect, therefore, that there should be an empirical relationship between concepts of democracy and the amount and quality of experience within democratic systems. Given the importance of the environment in Piaget's theory, egocentric concepts of democracy should be associated with little, and superficial, experience in democratic institutions. In Eastport this was in fact the case, as we shall see when we move on to the discussion of other measures of association.

Of Constitutions, Constituents, and Consent of the Governed

If for half of the Eastportians democracy *is* freedom, for the other half democracy and freedom stand together in a reciprocal relationship. Not only is there a clear differentiation between freedom and democracy, but democracy can be negated. The concept can be discussed in the abstract and applied to particular cases, and the principles of democracy can be derived from descriptions of concrete systems. Furthermore, democracy is actually practiced, in one form or another, by the Eastportians with sociocentric concepts of democracy.

In terms of content the sociocentric concepts of democracy contain the basic procedural principles of democracy, as shown in the following responses to the question "What is your understanding of democracy?":

> "A government of the people, by the people, and for the people. Freedom of the press, freedom of speech, freedom to go where you want. Elected officials, revolution, the Greek idea of democracy. . . . It is a form of government that allows you to do what you want to do, allows freedom, allows you representation";

"Democracy means to me that each individual has the right and the obligation to participate at whatever level in his government. . . . Each man has a vote, and each man has a way to register his like or dislike for something that's happening in the government";

"I guess my understanding of democracy would be a system whereby people get to elect the officials who represent them in both state and federal governments and through these elected officials the Constitution is implemented and carried out. Also, through these elected officials the basic needs of the people are met . . . through legislation. . . . It's a system of government that I think . . . basically . . . is determined by the general feelings of the people, the constituents."

Obviously, the concepts of democracy contained in these responses are not as fully developed as might be possible, but in comparison to the other half of Eastport, there is a world of difference. Here are views of democracy that entail cause and effect, principles of choice, and a differentiation between democracy as an operatory system of representation and democracy as a way of life. The responses are also examples of limited sociocentric concepts of democracy to the extent that they involve particularly "American" versions of democracy. The point, however, is that debate over issues of democratic practice would be facilitated by the fact that these Eastportians were dealing with abstractions and not comparing the merits of products in Persian and American supermarkets. In short, these Eastportians have an operatory concept of democracy. If presented with a problem requiring a democratic solution, they would have the necessary conceptual tools to provide a structure for arriving at a democratic solution.

Contributing Factors to the Dual Concepts of Democracy

Social circumstances, rather than family inheritances, seem to make the largest contribution to the two different structures underlying the idea of democracy in Eastport. The children do not fall into any particular pattern based on their fathers' concepts of democracy.

The children's concepts of democracy are distributed equally between concrete and operatory versions, regardless of the status of their fathers' concepts of democracy. It is also interesting to note that as a group the fathers had a far more adequate concept of democracy than their children. For example, on the content measure only three of the fifteen men failed to mention procedural principles of democracy. Some 80 percent of the fathers had operatory concepts of democracy, compared to 50 percent of the children.

Although there seems to be little paternal influence on the structure of the children's ideas of democracy, there are five other characteristics which rather dramatically differentiate the children in one conceptual group from those in the other: (1) education; (2) group memberships; (3) level of political activity; (4) electoral participation; and (5) level of moral reasoning. Each of these factors is an empirical association, and each can be directly linked to Piaget's theory of egocentrism.

Education

Of the sixteen children with egocentric concepts of democracy there were only three who had any schooling beyond high school; those three included two nurses and one man who attended broadcasting school for two years. Among the fourteen children with sociocentric concepts of democracy, only two did not have at least two years of college experience, and one of those two had taken college-level courses while in the military. Thus, those who understood democracy in terms of freedom and everyday life in America were the high-school-educated, while those who saw democracy as a decision-making procedure were the college-educated.

Obviously education is an important contributor to an understanding of democracy, both in terms of a higher likelihood of actual instruction in principles of democracy and in terms of education's contribution to cognitive development in general. Nevertheless, education should not be overemphasized. After all, the fathers were far less educated than the children (the fathers' average years of schooling completed was eight, and the children's fourteen), yet only one-fifth of the fathers failed to mention any democratic procedural

Table 1

Concept of democracy	High school education	College education
Egocentric	13	3
Sociocentric	2	12

$X^2 = 13.39$, 1 df, significant at $<.001*$

*As with all the chi-square tests reported, this is simply a ballpark figure of association insofar as the expected values are less than ten but greater than five, and since the degrees of freedom are so small.

principles, compared to half of the children. While education appears to be a major contributor (see table 1), the nature of that contribution is open to interpretation. Education is probably less important in people's learning *what* to think than in their learning *how* to think.

Education is important because it socializes people in such a manner that one must look for principles of justification for one's point of view; because it teaches people *how* to think; and because it places people in social positions in which they have greater access or potential access to democratic experience. It is this experience, both formal and informal, which accounts for the relatively fuller understanding of democracy among the college educated, or at least so it seems, based on the other factors associated with sociocentric versions of democracy.

In short, education alone is not enough, for we must have occasion to think about democracy in order to develop an adequate notion of the nature of democracy. Again, the strength of this interpretation is underlined by the fact that the fathers, who were far less educated but with substantially greater democratic experience, had a more operatory concept of democracy than the children.

Group Membership

Among the sixteen children who view democracy in terms of freedom and everyday life in America, only six belong to any formal membership group at all, and of those six, three are union members who belong to a union simply because it is a prerequisite for getting a job in their trade. They pay their dues but do not participate in union affairs. In contrast, among the fourteen children with an operatory concept of democracy, only three do *not* belong to a group (see table 2). Furthermore, five of those with an operatory concept of democracy have multiple group memberships. Among the groups to which the Eastportians with a sociocentric concept of democracy belong are a garden club, a bicycling association, a fraternity, bands, PTAS, a condominium association, an insurance professionals' organization, student government, church groups, a conservation group, a coaches' association, a faculty senate, and political groups. Three of these Eastportians are also union members, and they are far more active in union affairs than the union members in the group with an egocentric concept of democracy. Indeed, one of the union members in the operatory group was an important official in his white-collar union.

Just as Verba and Nie (1972) found that *any* group membership, even a bowling team, was a boost to political participation, group membership in Eastport is a boost to understanding democracy. Of course, in this case we cannot be sure if the arrow of causation is from behavior to concept, concept to behavior, or both. In theory, at least, organizational membership provides a window on group decision making. In the American culture such decision making generally includes some process of voting according to the principle of majority rule. Thus, group membership provides an experiential basis which either builds or reinforces a sociocentric concept of democracy. It is important to note in this context that whereas all

Table 2

Concept of democracy	Group membership	No group membership
Egocentric	6	10
Sociocentric	11	3

$X^2 = 5.14$, 1 *df, significant at* $<.03$

but Kuchinsky in the first generation belonged to some kind of association, almost half of the children have no group affiliation. This would seem to go some distance toward explaining the children's (as a generation) relatively less developed ideas of democracy compared to their fathers.

Political Activity

Closely related to group membership is the third distinguishing factor associated with the two concepts of democracy: level of political activity. In the group which equated democracy and freedom, political action was circumscribed. Seven of these sixteen people committed the following political acts (excluding voting, which is examined separately below): two people wrote letters to government officials (one on pay toilets, and one on blue laws); two people attended one local town meeting; one person checked off the box on his income tax return donating two dollars toward funding presidential elections; one person tried, and failed, to have a stop sign erected on his busy corner; one person tried, and failed, to have a mosquito-infested culvert near his home covered; and one person accompanied a friend to a scheduled meeting with the mayor which never transpired, and also donated a few hours' worth of typing skills to a mayoral candidate.

Among the fourteen people with sociocentric concepts of democracy, nine committed political acts, among which were the following: three people marched against the Vietnam War; two people were active in presidential campaigns; a union leader was responsible for lobbying the state legislature; a Young Americans for Freedom member participated actively in his campus charter; one man participated in a protest against ITT, mediated in a racial conflict at the school where he teaches, and has actively supported the women's movement on several occasions; one woman wrote dozens of letters to government officials (including a letter of condolence to Senator Thomas Eagleton when George McGovern dropped him as the vice-presidential choice in 1972), attended ward meetings, and circulated petitions on an issue of local concern; another woman was an assistant campaign manager in a race for a town council seat, and also wore McGovern campaign buttons and regularly signed petitions on political issues in her community; and one woman was active in the campaign to save whales from extinction. Clearly, both the level of political activity and the quality of political activity are dramatically different in these two groups of Eastportians. Thus, one's level of political activity and one's conceptualization of democracy seem to be related; but in what direction remains to be tested. That is, it is unclear if behavior influences concepts, or if concepts influence behavior.

The salient difference between the two groups' quality of political activity was that of individual versus group action. The political actions committed by those who equated democracy and freedom tended to be isolated, individual actions, while collective action tended to be much more prevalent in the group with an operatory concept of democracy. Protest marches, working in electoral campaigns, circulating petitions, union politics, and so forth, are group activities in which opportunities for social and political discourse, the testing of ideas and the need for their justification, are greater than in isolated acts of letter writing, donating two dollars toward presidential elections, or individually attempting to move a city bureaucracy to act on specific individual concerns. Collective activities encourage the exchange of ideas, communication of information, debate, and the consolidation of shared perspectives, and thus lead to more adequate concepts for use in political discourse. Piaget repeatedly emphasized that peers were the major stimulant to cognitive development. It would seem, then, that even for adults the same principle applies (see table 3).

Electoral Behavior

The fourth basic difference between the two conceptual groups has to do with voting behavior. The one form of democratic participation which is open to every citizen—voting—is a responsibility that over a third of the interviewed Eastportians had rejected or ignored. The consequence is that they did not have even the handle of voting with which to grasp the concept of democracy. Of course, voting is the *minimalist* form of political participation, but it nevertheless

Table 3

Political activity	Egocentric concept of democracy	Sociocentric concept of democracy
None	2	5
Individual	7	0
Collective	5*	9

$X^2 = 9.61$, 2 df, significant at $<.01$

*Included in collective action are the individuals who tried to cover over the culvert and to erect a stop sign, since even though they acted alone they had to confront and try to persuade government officials. The other three are those who attended a town meeting or accompanied a friend to an attempted meeting with the mayor.

has a significant influence on whether one views democracy in egocentric or sociocentric terms. There were only two nonvoters among those with a sociocentric concept of democracy, while the majority of those with egocentric concepts of democracy were nonvoters (see table 4).

Lane found that a major palliative against the feeling of powerlessness among Eastport's first generation was the men's electoral participation. Voting provided the men with a sense that they were participating in the creation of government and that the government was therefore their own. I would suggest further that their electoral activity provided them with an experiential handle with which to grasp the concept of democracy. The men mentioned voting more often than their children because in the men's lives, on the whole, voting (and not just in government elections but in the informal associations to which the men belonged) was more salient. The act

Table 4

Concept of democracy	Voters	Nonvoters
Egocentric	7	9
Sociocentric	12	2

$X^2 = 5.47$, 1 df, significant at $<.02$

of voting not only provides the voter a modicum of political power, it provides an experiential basis for the concept of democracy. Voting, therefore, contributes to an abstract, operatory concept of democracy.

Moral Reasoning

The final characteristic distinguishing the two groups takes us out of the more familiar territory upon which discussions of democracy generally take place and into an area that is more speculative but, nevertheless, potentially fruitful. The underlying hypothesis which guided this investigation is that political beliefs are structured by precisely the same cognitive operations which structure all other realms of experience. The way we learn about and conceptualize democracy, freedom, equality, government, power, and any number of other political phenomena is not unlike the way we learn about time, space, speed, causality, numbers, or other categories of physical experience. A major difference may be that our basic concepts that enable us to understand the physical world develop slowly and over an extended period of time as we travel our path to maturity, while our understanding of political concepts may develop more rapidly. Alternatively, it may be that our political concepts and our physical concepts do in fact develop at a similar rate and depend equally upon our experience; that is, from childhood, through adolescence, to adulthood, concepts of freedom, democracy, equality, and so forth, go through a series of stage-wise developments, each stage characterized by a particular equilibrium between perception and cognition.

The question of the rate of development, indeed of development itself, is a question for further research, but one purpose of this study was to examine political beliefs to determine if such research would be justified and if it would have relevance to adult ideologies.[4] One way to make that judgment is to use a measure directly related to cognitive development. Thus, we asked each of the subjects to respond to Kohlberg's moral reasoning scale, and we had the responses scored by Kohlberg's associates at Harvard's Graduate School of Education.

Moral reasoning and cognitive functioning are two different processes, and this should not be forgotten in what follows; but neither are they unrelated. Consequently, when it turned out that the children of Eastport were divided on the question of democracy in almost the same manner as they were divided on Kohlberg's scale, the hypothesized link between political reasoning and cognitive and moral development seemed justified (albeit in a *very* rough fashion). If the children's scores on Kohlberg's scale are divided arbitrarily into a group of fourteen high scorers and a group of sixteen low scorers, and these two groups are superimposed on the two groups distinguished by the four operationalized measures of egocentrism, there are only three misplaced people on each side of the dividing line. The people who scored higher on Kohlberg's scale were the people who viewed democracy as a decision-making process, and the people who scored lower on Kohlberg's scale were those who equated democracy with freedom and the American way of life (see table 5).

It should be emphasized that the measurement of moral development is an *indirect* measure of cognitive development, although there is a fairly basic relationship between high levels of cognitive functioning and high levels of moral reasoning: "The empirical relations found are that a given logical stage *is a necessary but not sufficient* condition for the parallel moral stage." (Kohlberg, 1973, p. 187.) Furthermore, "while moral stages are not simply special applications of logical stages, logical stages must be *prior* to moral stages, because they are more general." (Kohlberg, 1971a, p. 187.) Therefore, a study using levels of moral development to assess lev-

Table 5

Concept of democracy	High scores on Kohlberg's scale	Low scores on Kohlberg's scale
Egocentric	3	13
Sociocentric	11	3

$X^2 = 10.7$, 1 *df*, significant at <.01

els of cognitive development is bound to contain a margin of error that would lead, in the instance at hand, to the inclusion of some sociocentric individuals in the egocentric group.

Conclusion

Two distinct ways of conceptualizing democracy were found in Eastport. The concrete, egocentric perspective resulted in the confusion of everyday life in America with the general principles of democracy, while the abstract, sociocentric perspective recognized the procedural principles of democracy, differentiated democracy in relation to other political concepts, and viewed democracy in systemic rather than particularistic terms. The perspectives were identified on the basis of four criteria, including: (1) a content-based criterion which determined whether or not procedural principles of democracy were employed in the subjects' general discussion of democracy; (2) two criteria based on manipulation of the logic of democracy, which included the ability to negate democracy and the presence or absence of reversibility between concrete applications and abstract principles of democracy; and (3) an environmental/behavioral criterion which ascertained the degree of exposure to democratic processes. Five variables differentiated the two conceptual camps: (1) level of education; (2) group memberships; (3) level and quality of political activity; (4) electoral participation; and (5) level of moral reasoning.

In the next chapter we take a broader look at political reasoning. Instead of focusing on a single concept, we examine the manner in which people make sense of the political world in general.

Types of Thought and Forms of Political Reasoning: A Neo-Piagetian Analysis

This chapter focuses on how people reason and the consequences this has for their understanding of political and non-political phenomena. Two key claims are made: (1) that there is a general structure to an individual's reasoning—one which underlies his or her understanding of both physical and political events; (2) that the nature of this cognitive structure may vary from person to person, and therefore different people may understand their environment, both physical and political, in fundamentally different ways. These two hypotheses are tested by examining how people make sense of physical phenomena, such as an oscillating pendulum or a chemical reaction, and political phenomena, such as the American-Iranian hostage crisis of 1980. The quality of their reasoning is explored by using a variety of techniques including Piaget's "clinical experimentation," in-depth open-ended interviewing, and survey questions. There are certain caveats attached to the use of the last, and these are discussed later. Throughout, analysis focuses on the structure of the individuals' understanding. The results of the study provide strong support for both hypotheses.[1]

Piaget and Beyond

The approach adopted in this chapter is a structural developmental one. Although it follows in the Piagetian tradition sketched in chapter three, there are two key points of divergence. The first reflects differences in emphasis on the earlier and later periods of Piaget's work. Chapter three, following Piaget's earlier work, utilizes the concept of egocentricism as a key to the analysis of development. Similarly, as Piaget began by studying the development of the a priori qualities of reason enumerated by Kant, chapter four focuses on individual political concepts. Going further, it speculates that the development of these concepts may be uneven and that political conceptualization will lag behind development in other conceptual domains. In the present chapter, the approach adopted is more strongly influenced by the later Piaget, and therefore emphasizes the operational quality of reasoning and the general structure of the understanding it generates. The result is a concept of thinking which is compatible with the notion of egocentrism, but which offers a more encompassing theoretical vision.

Focusing on the operational nature of thinking, the concept of thinking presented in this chapter provides a basis both for explicating the quality of reasoning which gives rise to the various forms of egocentrism and for going beyond an analysis of egocentrism to a consideration of other dimensions of thinking. Adopting this more structural view, it may be argued that the quality of reasoning exists independently of the object of thought and may be clearly distinguished from it. This suggests that there is a general structure to an individual's thinking which will remain the same across various content domains. Of specific interest here, it suggests that a person's thinking about political matter shares a common structure with his or her thinking about other classes of phenomena, such as the social or physical.[2]

A second point of divergence reflects more than differing interpretations of Piaget's theory. Chapter four draws on Piaget for the purpose of analyzing politics. In so doing, it offers interesting insight into people's understanding of such central notions as freedom and democracy. At the same time it leaves Piagetian theory intact. Here we begin with the belief that although Piaget's work is seminal and provides a critical step in the direction of a better conception of reasoning, it falls short in certain respects. Most important, it is limited by a too narrow and undifferentiated understanding of social environments and by a failure to appreciate fully the role of these environments in the individual's construction of meaning.

Although the argument here is a theoretical one, it may be introduced by a consideration of evidence, gathered by Piagetian researchers, which suggests that Piaget's theoretical account of the dynamics of cognitive development is inadequate. Piaget's equilibrium theory maintains that cognitive development is fueled simultaneously by subjective demands for organization that are inherent in a person's constructive activity, and by practical demands for accommodation that are inherent in a person's exchange with an objective world. In Piaget's view these two sets of demands parallel one another and are only satisfied by the reasoning and practice produced by formal operational thought. As a result, all cognitive development is forced to this end point. The speed of development may vary across cultures, but the order and end of its progress do not. The problem here is that a considerable body of cross-cultural research, followed later by work on American adults, indicates that this theory-driven conclusion is incorrect. Many adults never reach formal operational thought. Indeed, some never reach the concrete operational stage. Piaget never adequately addressed this problem.[3]

In our view this failure to develop fully is likely to prove quite common. The data reported in this chapter and chapter three as well as later research reported by Rosenberg (1987, 1988a) suggest as much. This failure to develop and the resulting structural differences in how adults think requires a basic reworking of Piaget's theory. What is needed is a better understanding of social environments and the role they play in individuals' cognitive development. In other words, Piaget's rather narrowly psychological theory needs to be complemented by more careful sociological considerations. Amending Piaget's theory in light of these considerations, this chapter introduces a more differentiated concept of social environments and posits a greater role for those environments in the construction of meaning.

Although Piaget devotes most of his attention to the analysis of the individual and his or her interaction with the physical environment, he has on occasion elaborated a view of society and its role in development. In so doing, he considers two aspects of social life: the surface reality of its specific behavioral interactions and cultural practices; and the more essential reality of its general exchange structure. In the first regard he recognizes that cultures vary enormously in the specific demands and opportunities they present, but suggests that the consequences for individuals' cognitive development are minimal. Variation in cultural beliefs and practices may influence the rate of development, that is, the speed with which individuals typically move through the stages, but they will not alter its basic sequence or conclusion.

In Piaget's view it is that second aspect of social life, the general structure, not the specifics of a given culture, which most importantly affects individual cognitive development. In his analysis of this structure, Piaget focuses on the exchange between individuals. He argues that the success and maintenance of interpersonal exchange require that each individual coordinate his or her action with the other. To use his word, they must "co-operate." It is by virtue of this structural requirement of "co-operation" that society most powerfully enters the process of subjective meaning-making. In essence, its demand for interpersonal coordination creates cognitive demands (e.g., taking the perspective of the other and rule-following) that force individual development. Like the objective environment, the social environment serves to undermine subjective understandings whose structure is incompatible with its own. Insofar as the individual does not comprehend the social exchange in a manner compatible with its structure, his or her intentions will be frustrated and anticipations denied in the course of participating in daily social life. This will force a transformation in his or her thinking. According to Piaget, the cognitive demands of social exchange are such that they can be fully satisfed only when the individual is able to think in a formal operational manner.[4]

This conception of the structure of social life is limited in three important respects. First, it is conceived in basically dyadic or interpersonal terms. There is no consideration of how the exchange between individuals is articulated in the larger structures which constitute an entire society, culture, and polity, nor is there any recognition of how these larger structures may determine the essential qualities of interpersonal exchange. Second, and related to the first,

Piaget's conception of the structure of social life is based on the assumption that all social interactions are essentially the same. It does not consider the possibility that forms of social "co-operation," all of which involve role-taking and stable patterns of exchange, may vary either across societies or within a single society. Third, the role of society in the development of meaning is conceived in negative terms. It serves only to deny subjective constructions which are incompatible with it. There is no consideration of the collective definition of meaning and the positive role it may play in the individual's constructive activity.

Here we adopt a view of social environments which is less individualistic and more differentiated. First of all, we assume that the social exchange between individuals occurs in a larger societal context and is best understood accordingly. This context has its own inherent structure, one which determines the formal qualities of the kinds of social interaction and cultural discourse which occur within its boundaries. On this basis, we argue that social pressures for cognitive development must be understood in collective as well as dyadic terms. The importance of this claim becomes clearer when viewed in the context of our second assumption: that the structure of social life may vary across historical periods, societies, and even parts of the same society, Together, these two assumptions have important and unconventional implications for Piagetian psychology. Most fundamental, they suggest that the essential structure of social discourse and exchange, the force which compels individual cognitive development, will vary. Consequently, we would expect that structurally different sociocultural contexts would foster different levels of individual development. We would therefore expect adults living in these different contexts to think in fundamentally different ways.

Adopting this macrostructural view, we also assume that social environments play a more central role in the individual's construction of meaning. Inherent in the macro-social view is an assumption that societies are in some sense self-constituting. While dependent on individuals' action for its reproduction, society is itself a constructive force and thus creates its own level of meaning. It defines terms of existence which, even if related to individuals' definitions, are its own. In so doing, society contributes to the individual's construction of meaning not only in the negative ways elaborated in Piagetian theory, but in positive ways as well. In the latter regard it provides observable patterns of exchange and terms of discourse which not only deny individuals' understandings, but guide the development of more adequate ones. Given the incompatible structure of a developing individual's thinking, these culturally provided models will be misconceived initially. Nevertheless, the individual can, through imitation and learning, come to use them to guide his or her reasoning under conditions similar to those of initial learning. In the process this socially structured understanding is incorporated into the individual's consciousness and practice. It is recognized and serves to orient the individual's efforts to understand.

This redefinition of the dynamics of meaning-making also has important consequences for cognitive developmental analysis. At issue here is the definition of a given moment or stage in development. In the Piagetian view, a stage begins with the construction of a new way of thinking. In this first phase, an individual recognizes new aspects of the world but is unable to coordinate them in thought or action. Understanding at this point is fragmented and piecemeal. The stage stabilizes in a second phase, when experience of a domain leads to a coordination of understanding at this level. For purposes of static description of a structure of thinking, these two phases are linked. Thus, it is assumed that, depending on the subject matter, a person will think in either the uncoordinated terms of the first phase or the coordinated terms of the second. In light of our reconceptualization this conception of a stage and its attendant definition of a structure of thought have to be redefined. Piaget's second phase, that of coordinated understandings, necessarily gives the individual access to cultural definitions and allows a new level of recognition. Of course, the individual's ability to use these definitions to guide his or her own thinking is limited. Recognition is the product of observation made possible by subjective coordination, but it is not itself subjectively coordinated. Recognized cultural definitions or models are therefore understood only as they are observed to apply in specific situations. Within this limit, the individual's capacity to reason is extended. He or she is able to reason not only according to subjectively coordinated understandings, but also along the lines suggested by these newly recognized culturally provided definitions. In our view the latter is a natural consequence of the former. This requires a redefinition of what constitutes a stage of development. Put in terms of Piagetian definitions, thinking stabilizes not at a point encompassing phase one and phase two of subjective coordination, but rather at a point encompassing phase two of a given coordination and phase one of the one which will follow. This argument is reflected in our redefinition of the stages of thinking.

In sum, the analysis of political thinking that we offer not only represents a response to the belief systems approach criticized in chapter two, it also reflects an attempt to improve on the Piagetian alternative elaborated in chapter three. In the latter regard it adopts a more social psychological conception of development. In so doing, it provides a better way of understanding the empirical data with which we began this dicussion, the data which suggested that not all adults think in a formal operational manner. While representing an anomalous or counter-theoretical result when viewed from the classic Piagetian position, this kind of evidence is wholly consistent with the modified version of the theory offered here. By viewing social exchange in a macro-social structure context, and by recognizing that the structure of this context may vary, we are led to the conclusion that not all adults will reach the same stage of development, the formal operational stage. Rather, it is to be expected that adult members of structurally different environments will develop to differing degrees and therefore think and understand in fundamentally different ways. Our neo-Piagetian view also leads to a modification in the definition of the forms of thinking themselves.

The Structural Developmental Approach

Thus far, the approach adopted in the present chapter has been presented in light of the discussion of Piaget's theory in chapter three. Here, we present this structural developmental approach in its own terms. The theory on which this approach is based has been developed in the work of a number of cognitive psychologists. Two rather different theoretical traditions have emerged: one following the more structural orientation of Jean Piaget (Piaget, 1970a, 1970b, 1977; Kohlberg, 1969, 1981; Selman, 1975; Kegan, 1982) and the other following the more dialectical tradition of L. S. Vygotsky (Vygotsky, 1974; Luria, 1976; Riegel and Rosenwald, 1975; Youniss, 1978). While there are significant differences among these research traditions, there is a more or less common understanding of reasoning which informs all of them.

The structural developmental view of cognition is based on two key assumptions. The first is that an individual's thought is structured and, therefore, constitutes a coherent unity. Its coherence is a result of the activity of thinking itself. According to the structural developmental view, thinking consists of the individual's attempt to operate upon the world and then understand (integrate or assimilate) the effects that his or her attempt achieves. Through this operatory activity, objects come to be regarded and manipulated (either physically or mentally). Expectations are established and then are confirmed or rejected. As the medium of the individual's exchange with the environment, thinking determines the structure of that individual's experience. One's capacity to operate (the manner in which one thinks) delimits both the nature of what one can experience (the quality of the possible objects of one's thought) and how one will organize those experiences (the type of analytical relations that one may establish between objects). It is in this sense that the individual's thought is assumed to be coherent.

This first assumption, that of the structured and coherent quality of an individual's thought, underlies the highly subjectivist and psychological element of structural developmental theory. It is a characteristic of the individual, his or her mode of thinking or capacity to operate, which determines the nature of the individual's experience. Although the substance of experience is provided by an external reality, the structure of that experience—the qualities of its constituent elements and the relations which exist among them—is a product of the individual's own subjective construction. When interacting with the environment the individual necessarily imposes the formal properties of his or her way of thinking (the qualities of the elements defined and the relations established) on the experience of the interaction. Thus, the definition and organization of experience is more a matter of subjective, rather than objective, determination.

In its structuralist subjectivism this conception of thinking is quite different from the conception underlying belief systems research. In the latter tradition a belief system is defined as a constrained set of "idea-elements." These "idea-elements" or attitudes are assumed to have some meaning independent of the belief system in which they are incorporated, and the constraint among the elements of the belief system is explained in terms of social influences. In this vein the belief systems research is oriented by the assumption that thinking is basically a recognitory and associative exercise. Thinking is understood to be guided by actual or reported relations between real or socially defined objects. In contrast to this view of thinking, the structural developmental conception suggests that both the nature of the associations a person makes and the quality of the objects so associated are determined by the underlying structure of that person's thought.

The second basic assumption underlying the structural developmental view is that cognition develops. Like its structure, the development of cognition is understood to be a necessary result of the activity of thinking itself. Thinking is a fundamentally pragmatic activity: it arises in the course of interaction with the environment and yields a guide to further interaction. It provides the individual with a knowledge of how to act and what to expect. The individual then directs future behavior accordingly. In so doing, the individual relates his or her understanding to the realities of the environment. While the individual's action is subjectively directed, it takes place in an objective world. Therefore, the individual's action is necessarily regulated by rules which are inherent in the environment in which he or she acts. Given these objective limitations on action, the individual's understanding (as the guide to and reflection upon action) necessarily is constrained by the structure of that individual's environment.

The claim that personal experience is environmentally as well as subjectively structured is critical to the developmental view of cognition. It is the interaction between these two structuring forces, subjective and objective, which constitutes the developmental dynamic. To the extent that the individual's construction of experience is inconsistent with the real constraints imposed on that experience by the environment, the individual's understanding of the world will prove unreliable. Self-directed action will end in failure and unexpected outcomes will be frequent. These failures and unexpected outcomes give rise to a sense of confusion and self-doubt. The individual begins to wonder about the adequacy of his or her understanding of the world. Concern shifts from what one knows to how one knows; the individual reflects.

What does this reflection involve? On the one hand, it involves building on the rejected terms of prior understanding. The conceptual relations characteristic of the rejected understanding become the objects of reflection. As a result, reflection is not arbitrary. Rather, it is determined, in part, by the old understanding being objectified and transcended. On the other hand, reflection involves the construction of a new mode of thinking. The act of taking one's way of understanding as object entails the consideration of an object of thought which is not constructed in the course of one's normal thinking. As such, the consideration of this new object prefigures the emergence of a new mode of thinking—one which includes this new object within its normal range of operation. With the elaboration of this new mode of thinking, the structure of thought is transformed and experience is reconstructed. New objects are defined and new kinds of relations among them are forged. Considering both aspects of this reflective activity together, we see that the change engendered is at once directed (the new is built upon the old) and fundamental (the structure of thought is transformed).

In sum, thinking is embedded in an ongoing process of subjective construction, denial, reflection and reconstruction. Stepping back from the process, we see that cognition is basically a developmental phenomenon. By its nature, cognitive functioning leads to a series of transformations in the individual's way of thinking. With each transformation a new stage of development is introduced. The dynamic of this development is such that the overall progress has the following characteristics. First, because each stage builds on the preceding stage and creates the foundation of the succeeding stage, the order of development will not vary across persons. Second, because each stage emerges as a reflective response to the inadequacies of thought at the preceding stage, development leads both to an ever greater cognitive sophistication and to a more appropriate adaptation to the environment. Third, because environments stimulate development and the structure of environments may vary, different individuals may achieve different levels of development.

By introducing this second assumption, that of development, it is important to note that we complement the subjectivist and psychological emphases of our structuralist view with environmental and sociological considerations. The result is a view of thinking which is at once strongly psychological and strongly sociological. The view is strongly psychological in two respects. It asserts: (1) that thinking is a personal activity which yields a subjectively constructed understanding and, therefore, that the structural qualities of an individual's cognitive functioning will be independent of the particular situations that individual confronts; and (2) that insofar as the structure of thought varies across individuals, different people may have fundamentally different understandings of their social and political environments. At the same time the view presented here is strongly sociological. This is true in that it asserts: (1) that the structure of the environment may force structural transformations in how an individual thinks; and (2) that the variation in the structure of environments will cause variation in the level of development individuals will achieve and, therefore, will create fundamental differences in how people think. In sum, the structural developmental perspective offers a deeply social psychological view of the nature of cognition.

The Design and Method of Empirical Research

The structural developmental theory of cognition dictates the aims and, thereby, the design of empirical research on political reasoning. As suggested by the theory, the aims of empirical research are (1) to determine the nature of the various forms which thinking may take; and (2) to discover the conditions which lead to the emergence of these forms. The first aim sets the descriptive goals of the research. The structure (the conceptual relations and units) of each thought form must be described and the political understanding that structure yields must be analyzed. The second aim, the discovery of the conditions of the emergence of thought forms, sets the explanatory goals of the research. The impact of environments on the construction of understanding must be determined. To this end the researcher must construct a relevant typology of environments and then establish how different kinds of environments facilitate or inhibit the progress of cognitive development.

These goals dictate the design of structural developmental research. Exploring the structural qualities of thought requires (1) that the investigation focus on individual subjects (rather than focusing on aggregate data); and (2) that each subject be required to perform a number of different tasks (to allow a relatively context-free assessment of cognitive functioning). Analyzing the conditions of structural transformation requires (1) that the thought of individual subjects be examined over a period of years; and (2) that the effect of differently structured environments on both subjects' current thinking and their long-term development be studied.

Like the research design, the methods of research reflect the dictates of structural developmental theory. As noted in chapter one, the assumptions that thought is structured and that individual differences do exist suggest that the research task is quite similar to that of the historian of philosophy. The task confronting the historian of philosophy is to determine how a particular philosopher thinks. Aware that the philosopher may think in a quite distinctive way, the historian approaches the task of interpretation so as to avoid reducing the terms of the philosopher's thought to his or her own. The historian accomplishes this task first by examining a number of the philosopher's assertions and arguments. He or she then builds a model of the philosopher's thought which will make sense of these assertions. Only when these assertions and others made by the philosopher are rendered coherent does the historian feel comfortable with his or her interpretation.

The researcher working in the structural developmental tradition regards his or her subjects as lay philosophers. Like the historian of philosophy, the researcher attempts to build an interpretive model of the subjects' thought. Unlike the historian, the researcher must begin by making subjects speak. Recognizing that any single attitude or action may mean many things and, therefore, may be misinterpreted easily, the researcher uses empirical methods (e.g., open-ended interviews or clinical experimentation) that give subjects the opportunity to reason at length about specific problems or issues. In this context the researcher also probes subjects' reasoning to clarify the nature of the connections they are making. In this manner the researcher ensures that the data collected are sufficiently rich—that the subject has made a sufficient number of related claims—to allow for the construction of an interpretive model of the subject's thought.

In the research reported here we present an empirical study which both exemplifies the structural developmental approach and offers evidence of its value. It is worth noting that our research is rather different from much of the research in this tradition, in several respects. First, the research reported here adopts a different focus from that adopted in most of the structural developmental research. The structural developmental research emerged almost exclusively as a response to learning and socialization theories (e.g., Piaget, 1965; Kohlberg, 1969). Almost all of the research has been conducted on children and focuses on issues of the invariance of the developmental sequence. The research presented here emerges in response to the research on adult reasoning. As a result, the work has been conducted on adults and focuses on the issue of structural differences in cognition which exist among adults.

Second, much of the American and West European research follows in the Piagetian tradition. Thus, it has emphasized the structural and psychological qualities of thought. The research reported here is part of a larger effort to go beyond this tradition. Thus, an attempt is made to define concepts in light of the relationship between the psychological and sociological bases of meaning. This concern is reflected in the definition of the types of thought structures presented here. This is true in two respects: (1) structures of thought are described in the language of action and interaction rather than in the language of mathematics; and (2) the intrasubjective (or psychological) and the intersubjective (or social) regulations of thought are viewed as related dimensions of cognitive structure.

Third, although failing to offer a theoretical justification for the move, much of the structural developmental research has adopted a division of the area of inquiry according to the kinds of problems the individual addresses. Thus, some researchers study reasoning about physical phenomena, others study reasoning about social phenomena, and still others study reasoning about moral phenomena. Here, the concern is with political phenomena. This not only leads structural developmental research into a new arena, but also raises questions about an individual's thinking across domains. Political considerations are social and moral as well as strictly governmental. Consequently, the study of political thinking forces us to examine how an individual reasons across domains heretofore considered distinct. This has led the research presented here in two new directions: (1) to define the structure of thinking in a way that is free of specific social, moral, or political content and that is therefore appropriate to the characterization of thought of all three types; and (2) to examine an individual's thinking across substantively differentiated domains (e.g., the physical, social, and political).

Finally, we attempt to demonstrate directly the relevance of the structural developmental approach to the more mainstream belief systems research. This is done by using information gathered through appropriate structural developmental methods to predict subjects' responses to conventional survey items. There are strong theoretical and methodological reasons for proceeding very cautiously. It is difficult both to translate the concerns of one epistemological framework into another and to compare sets of data gathered with different methodological considerations in mind. Nevertheless, there are pragmatic reasons for making such an attempt. The best way to demonstrate the value of an alternative perspective is to use it in the analysis of familiar kinds of data.

In applying structural developmental theory to the study of political thinking, we first define the nature of thinking which emerges at three stages of development. The three types of thought described are sequential, linear, and systematic. In light of the need for a very general definition of the structural qualities of each type of thought, each of the three types is defined initially in abstract terms. Then, the particular way of reasoning about politics associated with each type of thought is described. Having offered our theoretical definitions, we then report empirical research. The theory presented is very broad in scope. Consequently, the empirical study reported here must be regarded as a first step in a long-term program of research.

Definition of Three Types of Political Reasoning

Here, three types of political reasoning are described. They are sequential, linear, and systematic. True to their conception, each type of political reasoning is described first in terms of its constitutent structure and then with regard to the social and political understanding that structure engenders. The typology presented here reflects a number of influences. On the one hand, it has been influenced by a critical reading of the epistemological writings of G. W. F. Hegel and the psychological theorizing of Jean Piaget, Lawrence Kohlberg, and L. S. Vygotsky. On the other hand, it has been influenced by our own preliminary research and the opportunity to review some data collected by Piaget and Kohlberg.[5]

When reviewing the description of the various types of political reasoning, it is important to keep in mind that an attempt is made to define the underlying structure of thought. This structure determines both the manner and object of an individual's reasoning. This does not suggest, however, that the individual will not be able to address additional concerns. Given the appropriate exposure and training, an individual may learn to apply analytical strategies and to consider objects which are not natural products of his or her own thought structure. Despite these specific learning experiences, the individual lacks the cognitive structure to support these new concepts. Consequently, his or her ability to use them will be limited. Learned strategies will only be applied in the contexts in which they were initially learned, and learned objects will be redefined in a manner consistent with the structure of the individual's thought. While these limits may not be observed easily in day-to-day discourse, they become apparent when individuals are asked either to clarify the meaning of their statements or to analyze novel situations or problems.

Sequential Thought

Sequential thinkers track the world which appears before them. Their focus is on the immediate and specific events that they observe. They understand these events as moments in an unfolding sequence. The questions which guide their intellectual activity are: What does what I see look like? What will follow? Sequential thinkers find the answers to their questions through their own observations of what occurs before them.

The structure of sequential thought. Thinking by tracking determines the conceptual relations and units of sequential thought. The conceptual relations of sequential thought are synthetic without being analytic. The connections they create are not so much distinct links between separate entities as a fusion of these entities with the links which connect them. Thus, neither the links between entities nor the entities themselves have independent analytical status. Constituted in this manner, the relations of sequential thought have three distinctive qualities. First, these conceptual relations are perceptually mediated. Consequently, their form reflects the processes of observation and representation. Thus, they consist of either sequential orderings (reflecting the observed connection of a series of events) or recognitory matches (reflecting the matching of current observation with the representation of earlier observation). Second, the conceptual relations of sequential thought are concrete and specific. Because these relations are not analytically independent of the entities observed, they are embedded in observed sequences of events. As a result, they are not abstract, do not facilitate generalization and do not support metaphorical thinking. Third, the relations of sequential thought are quite mutable. Bound to observed events, these relations will change as observation requires. Thus, although a learned sequential relation engenders a sense of anticipation, it is readily transformed by new experience. In addition, a learned sequential relation can be extended or integrated with other learned sequences which share overlapping events.

The conceptual units of sequential thought consist of currently observed or once observed objects. These observed objects are understood in two ways. On the one hand, they may be understood in terms of their place in a sequence. In this context the objects of sequential thought are conceived as events or moments. On the other hand, observed objects may be understood by their relation to representations of earlier observations. In this frame of reference the objects are conceived as recognitions or novelties.

Understanding the physical world. The world of the sequential thinker is concrete, proximate, and fluid. The space of that world is constituted by the events that the sequential thinker observes and by the images that those events call forth. There is no place for observable events not yet observed, nor for unobservable phenomena. If another person introduces these foreign concerns, either they will not be understood and will, therefore, be ignored, or they will be reduced to the terms of sequential thought and will, therefore, be misunderstood. The time of the sequential thinker's world is one of a passing present. Past and future are not clearly distinguished. By its appearance or another person's suggestion a current event may cue the consideration of a past or anticipated event. Once considered, the temporally removed event becomes part of the sequential thinker's present circumstances.

Understanding politics. The social and political universe of the sequential thinker tends to be immediate both in space and time. It consists of the flow of currently observed and represented events. These events are ordered with regard to the sequence in which they are observed to occur. They are not viewed with reference to nonpresent influences or governing rules of interaction. Consequently, the environment conceived by the sequential thinker does not properly include such forces as intention, power, norm, or law. So constituted, the social universe is not clearly differentiated from the physical world; events of both types are intermingled.

The participants in these action sequences are observed, or once observed and currently represented, individuals. These individuals are understood either in terms of their identity (a recognitory match) or in terms of their participation in a specific sequence of events (a sequential ordering). So conceived, individuals have only observable qualities—not any hidden or abstract ones such as motives, emotions, or thoughts. To the degree to which these unobservable qualities are considered, they are regarded as the accompaniments of action rather than as causes of significant independent status. At the same time individuals are understood only in the context of specific situations. Consequently, they are not given any global or cross-situational definition; they are not thought of as personalities. Similarly, individuals are not thought of in terms of any enduring relationship they bear to one another. As a result, social bonds such as marriage or group membership are not part of the sequential thinker's definition of persons.

The complex polity has a reality which is extended in space and time and is internally differentiated both vertically and horizontally. Consequently, exposure to such a polity presents sequential thinkers with a number of phenomena that they do not naturally address and cannot properly comprehend. Some of these phenomena are sufficiently abstract (e.g., nation-states, policy reform, legal principles) that they cannot really be introduced to sequential thought. These phenomena, therefore, may be ignored. If they are considered, they will be thought of in a way which renders them consistent with sequential thought. For example, consider the sequential thinker's understanding of such an abstract concept as a legal principle. This understanding emerges as follows. A law may forbid a specific action that the sequential thinker performs. The performance of this action leads to punishment, and the sequential thinker will not repeat the act. This does not imply, however, that he or she shares the legal community's conception of the law in question, as an expression of an underlying legal principle. Rather, the sequential thinker conceives of the law in his or her own terms—as an undesirable outcome following from a specific activity.

Linear Thought

Linear thinkers analyze action sequences. They focus on specific actions and attempt to determine the relations which exist among them. The questions which guide their intellectual activity are as follows: What caused an observed effect or what effect will an observed cause create? What is the relative impact of several causes which have a similar effect? What is the correct or proper sequence of actions which should take place? The answers to these questions are discovered through observation, one's own or another's.

The structure of linear thought. The conceptual relations of linear thought are unidirectional and atemporal. As such, these relations are somewhat independent of the units upon which they operate. So constituted, the conceptual relations of linear thought have several distinguishing characteristics: (1) Themselves unobservable, linear relations impose their unidirectional structure on the contents of observation. (2) The construction of any particular relation depends on perceived associations between observable units. Thus, the contents or substance of linear relations are derived from experience rather than from reflection. (3) Once constructed, linear relations have a limited generality. They are specific to the actions related, but generalize to whatever or whoever engages in those actions. (4) Linear relations assign priority to one of the units related. This priority unit then provides a basis for defining and comparing subordinate units which may be related to it.

The conceptual units of linear thought are actions. These action units have three important qualities. First, they are observable. That is, they include not only actions which are being observed, but also related actions which are not currently occurring. Second, these units are extensive. They reach beyond themselves and demand connection with at least one other unit. Third, several of these action units (past as well as present) may be held in the mind's eye simultaneously. Fourth, these units may be compared by virtue of their common relation to an additional unit. Thus, units may be categorized and ranked.

It should be noted that observed objects, the units of sequential thought, are reconstituted here as conceptual subunits. As subunits, they are not meaningful in themselves. Rather, they acquire definition by virtue of their involvement in action. Thus, these subunits are (1) conceived in action terms—that is, as actor or acted upon; (2) defined by the specific things they do or have done to them; and (3) observable, but need not ever be seen; their existence may be inferred from the consequence of their action.

Understanding the physical world. The world of the linear thinker is an extended one. Given the unidirectional quality of linear relations and the extensive quality of linear units, the observation of action leads to inferences about actions removed in space and time. Thus, the space of the linear thinker reaches beyond the proximate reality to include actions and objects not currently being observed. Built in part upon inferences from observed effects to unobserved causes, this space also includes supernatural or spiritual forces and actors (they may never be seen but are thought of as observable entities). The time of the linear thinker's world also extends beyond the immediate. Through a consideration of prior causes and consequent effects of current activity, past and future are constructed.

Several points are worth making about this extended universe. First, while larger than the proximate and current reality of the sequential thinker, the linear thinker's world extends out from that reality and, therefore, is oriented by it. As the substance of the immediate reality of the linear thinker changes, so will the extended space and time it calls forth. Second, the linear thinker's world is an ordered but fragmented one. Where links between actions are observed, relations are established and an order is created. However, where links are not observed, no relations are created. Consequently, understandings (and the realities they organize) are isolated from one another. Third, the linear thinker's world is regarded as given. Because the construction of relations depends on observed activity, the linear thinker does not complement his or her vision of what is with an idea of what might be.

Understanding politics. Linear thought consists of the analysis of the relations between specific actions. These relations themselves are not subject to analysis. Therefore, general categories of relations among actions (that is, interactions) are not defined. Consequently, the linear thinker does not differentiate between such categories of action as social and political. (When the environment requires such distinctions, the linear thinker will differentiate types of action on the basis of who performs them [e.g., political action is that action performed by politicians], not on the basis of the quality or function of the interactive context in which action occurs.) Thus, the linear thinker does not really distinguish politics from social life more generally.

The linear thinker's sociopolitical universe has several distinctive characteristics. First, it has a broad compass; it includes both temporally and spatially removed forces. Thus, the linear thinker naturally considers current events both in light of past causes and future effects and with regard to their relation to political actors and outcomes which are not a part of the immediate environment. Second, the linear thinker's sociopolitical universe has a shifting focus. That universe extends out from the linear thinker's proximate and current reality. Consequently, the linear thinker's conception of removed political concerns is oriented by present realities. As the substance of the immediate political reality changes, so will the removed time and space it calls forth. Third, the linear thinker's sociopolitical universe has an order. There is a specific and concrete rule or law which governs each social and political activity. Each activity has its effect, and each effect has its cause. It is presumed that these linkages will be sustained in the future. Therefore, when the unexpected occurs, there is surprise and an immediate search for an explanation. The search ends with the identification of the intervening force which is presumed to have caused the unanticipated outcome. Thus, there is no element of randomness in the linear thinker's understanding of political life. Fourth, the linear thinker's sociopolitical universe is regarded as given. Because the linear thinker constructs relations based on observed associations or others' reports, the linear thinker does not complement his or her observation of what is done with a conception of what might be done. If alternatives are to be considered, they must first be presented by other people. Fifth, the sociopolitical universe of the political thinker is a fragmented one. Where links among actions are observed or reported, relations are inferred. However, where no links are observed or reported, no relations are inferred. Consequently, the linear thinker's political universe consists of islands of relationships in a sea of unconsidered connections.

The linear thinker's political analyses focus on the observed relations which exist among people's actions. These relations then are understood in causal terms: one action causes or is caused by another action. The specific causal attributions made are oriented either by personal observation or by another's report. When the action which precedes a person's action is observed, the preceding action will be attributed causal force. When no prior action is observed, causal force will be attributed either to actions internal to the individual (e.g., drives, needs, or passions) or to spiritual forces (e.g., God's work or fate). When information is offered by others, it may determine how causality is attributed. It should be noted that a connection between actions may acquire the status of a norm or law. As conceived by the linear thinker, a norm provides a guide for correct behavior under a particular set of circumstances. So constituted, norms lead to the ritualization of political interaction.

Individuals are understood in terms of their relation to action. Thus, individuals are conceived of as actors and are distinguished by the specific things they do and have done to them. No integrated conception of the individual actor is formed. As suggested earlier, some of the individual's actions are seen to be internally motivated, the product of internal motive forces. Inferred from their observed action consequences, these motive forces are defined by the actions they are assumed to cause. Consequently, motives do not provide a context for the interpretation of the meaning of an action.

In addition to defining the intrinsic qualities of individuals, action also provides a basis for defining individual's social or political status. This may occur in two ways. On the one hand, individuals' status may be defined on the basis of how they act in interaction with others. These interactions are analyzed in causal terms, and the participants' social and political status is defined accordingly. Insofar as individuals are initiators of action, they are viewed as full participants in human affairs and are attributed commensurately high status. Insofar as individuals are mere followers of others' initiatives, they are regarded more as the objects than the subjects of social life. Therefore, they are attributed lower status. Thus, the linear analysis of social interaction leads to a conception of interpersonal relations which is hierarchical and a political definition of individuals which reflects their capacity to exercise personal power.

On the other hand, individuals' social and political status may also be defined in light of the relation of their action to the action of others. Individuals who perform the same action may be conceived to be of the same category. In this manner social groups are defined. These groups may be distinguished on the basis of common ritual, common location, common parentage, and common appearance.

Several points should be made regarding the manner in which political groups are understood. First, these groups are understood to be the sum of their members and are identified by those members' shared characteristics. Second, political groups are understood to be hierarchically organized. The leader is the source of power in the group and the personification of its unity. Third, when groups are considered relative to one another, each group is conceived of as a single undifferentiated actor. Therefore, in an intergroup context, the action of each group is conceived of in the same terms as the action of an individual political actor.

Systematic Thought

Systematic thinkers juxtapose the relationships which exist between actions. They analyze these relationships by examining them relative to one another, by considering each in its context. Thus, systematic thinkers recognize that a relationship they observe may be a product of either objective conditions or subjective associations. The relationship is interpreted and explained accordingly. Consequently, the intellectual activity of systematic thinkers is oriented by the following questions: What are the conditions under which an observed relationship will obtain? What are the rules which govern associations among observed relationships? What role or function does a given activity or interaction play in a system? In an argument, does a proposed relationship make sense? Does a proposed relationship match observed relationships that it is intended to describe? Systematic thinkers answer these questions in two ways. In the case of empirical questions they answer by recourse to systematic observation. Thus, they consider the conditions—subjective as well as objective—which may influence an observed relationship. In the case of theoretical questions they concern themselves with the connections among proposed relationships in light of such issues as necessity and noncontradiction.

The structure of systematic thought. The juxtapositional quality of their reasoning determines the kind of relations and units that systematic thinkers construct. The relations of systematic thought are bidirectional. So structured, systematic relations are not anchored in the definition of either unit, but rather constitute the association which exists between them. Various forms of association between units may be established (e.g., implication, identity, negation). In combination, systematic relations may delineate the multiple associations which exist among a set of units. In this manner an analytical system is constructed. So constituted, the relations of systematic thought have two key distinguishing characteristics. First, they provide a basis for interpretation. Any given unit then is analyzed in light of the system in which it is embedded. Second, systematic relations are regulative. Actions are presumed to be constrained by the system in which they are embedded.

The units of systematic thought consist of the relationships between actions (either observed or imagined). These relationships may be interactive or classificatory. In the case of interactive relationships, actions which co-occur are considered together. In the case of classificatory relationships, actions are considered in light of their impact on the system of which they are a part. Actions which have a similar outcome are regarded as members of a common class. (It should be noted that the actions which comprise these relationship-units are subunits and, therefore, are only understood with reference to their interactive or systematic context.) Both types of units, interactive and classificatory, have dual identities. On the one hand, they are defined by the systematic context in which they are embedded. On the other hand, they have an intrinsic meaning or identity which remains constant across the various relational contexts in which they are articulated.

In this structural context the construction of units and relations is complex. This is true in two senses. In part, construction is complicated by the fact that relations and units are independent of one another and, therefore, each has a conceptual primacy. The primacy of the relations is reflected by the systematic thinker's ability to make general claims (build theories) which order and define the units that they explain. The primacy of the units is reflected in the systematic thinker's assumption that all general claims, regardless of their theoretical origins, apply to a single, objective world of action (and thus share a common empirical ground). The construction of systematic units and relations is also complex in a second sense. This is a result of the fact that both units and relations share a common form; they are both bidirectional and associative. Consequently, the systematic thinker can regard a relationship between actions as either a unit or a relation. In so doing, the systematic thinker can construct relations at a number of levels of generality or inclusiveness. Each level is constructed by relating units which, at a lower level, are themselves relations among units.

Understanding the physical world. The physical world of the systematic thinker is integrated and rule-governed. It consists of a system of interconnected relationships. These define the rules of the system and serve as constraints on action. Although experience leads the systematic thinker to leave certain relationships unobserved or unconsidered, he or she retains the sense of the potential for those relationships. At the same time the world is differentiated into a number of domains or subsystems. These are distinguished either by the density of observed interconnections or by the type of function a class of activity serves in the larger system.

In this context the spatiotemporal parameters of systematic thought are constructed. Space is conceived as the multiple linkages which are operative at any moment in time. So constituted, this space is more than an extension beyond a proximate reality. Indeed, that proximate reality is itself defined as an element of that larger space and is analyzed accordingly. The time of systematic thought consists of a succession of periods. Each period is distinguished by the system of relationships which govern the action of that period. Change in these systems is understood to be the consequence of the spatial relations which either operate within the system or link the system to other systems. In this framework the past and future, while possessing links to the present, are defined as systems unto themselves.

Understanding politics. The systematic thinker reasons in terms of systems of interactions and functional classes of action. This engenders two of the most distinctive characteristics of the systematic thinker's understanding of politics. First, all political activity is understood to occur in a larger context. Observed interactions are interpreted and explained accordingly. Second, the political universe is divided into subsystems, and the activity in each subsystem may be differentiated into several functional classes. As a result of the construction of subsystems, social orders or societies are defined. Each is distinguished by the density of interconnections among the interrelated activities performed. As a result of the construction of functional classes, different types of behavior are defined. This provides a basis for differentiating politics from social activity generally. Thus, politics may be defined as that class of actions which is related to the governing of a social system.

The systematic thinker regards political phenomena from two perspectives. Each reflects a different placement of the locus of the system of actions being observed. On one hand, the systematic thinker focuses on the relationships which exist between actions performed by different people. Here, personal action is seen to be embedded in social interaction, and interactions are understood with reference to the systematic context in which they occur. The system of interactions among individuals constitutes a social organization. Those activities which perform the common function of maintaining the order and coordination of that organization are regarded as members of a common class. They define the political dimension of social life. Thus, politics is conceived in terms of the set of governing regulations—the set of institutions, laws and mores—which mediate these interactions. Power is understood to inhere in the political system itself, not in individuals. In sum, this first perspective generated by systematic thought is quite sociological.

It is important to note how individuals are conceived in this frame of reference. The key point is that individuals' actions are seen to be embedded in interaction with others. Therefore, an individual's action is understood to be a product not of his or her will, but rather of the interaction in which the individual is participating. Consequently, individuals are regarded in the following manner. First, they are presumed to be a product of their environment. The social environment or situation determines the specific attitudes or behaviors of the individuals in that environment. Second, all individuals are regarded as having equivalent social capacities. Anyone can be trained or socialized to perform the behaviors required by a particular environment. Individuals are, therefore, interchangeable placeholders in the political system. In this sense they are regarded as equal.

The systematic thinker may view human affairs in a second way, by focusing on the relationships which exist among a single person's actions. Here, it is not the interactive context but the individual which is the object of analytical concern. In this light the individual is understood in two ways. On the one hand, the individual is understood as a regulator, the source of coordination of his or her own thought and action. Thus the individual is understood to be a rational and purposive actor. On the other hand, the individual is understood in terms of his or her characteristic manner of interaction with others; that is, in terms of interactive personality traits (e.g., withdrawal, cooperation, leadership). The individual is understood by the aggregate or set of these traits. In both of these conceptions the individual is regarded as a free agent, the director of action and the organizer of thoughts. The individual's interactions with others are understood to be a product of each person's desires and intentions. In this respect this second view of political life is quite psychological.

In considering these two perspectives generated by systematic thought, it is clear that there are certain incompatibilities. These incompatibilities define one of the characteristic tensions of systematic thought: the tension between the sociological focus of the first vision and the psychological focus of the second; between the social determinism of the first vision and the free will orientation of the second.

The Empirical Research

Here, we explore a number of our structural developmental hypotheses. The two central hypotheses:

(1) Different individuals think in fundamentally different ways. These differences are structural. Therefore, even when confronted with the same simple, clearly defined problem, different individuals may think about that problem in fundamentally different ways. That is, they may think about the problem in a sequential, linear, or systematic fashion.

(2) Given the subjectively structured nature of his or her thought, the same individual will think about very different things in the same structurally determined manner. Therefore, the individual's political reasoning should reflect the same structural qualities as his or her reasoning about social and physical phenomena.

The third hypothesis speaks to the relation between the structure of the individual's thought and his or her responses to survey questions generally used by political scientists. The survey questions used in investigating the third hypothesis are drawn from survey instruments used in most of the research on public opinion and voting behavior. Again, a caveat must be introduced. Because of the different methodological considerations governing the development of a survey instrument, the following hypothesis is advanced tentatively and more for the purpose of illustrating the value of our approach than for validating its claims.

(3) Individuals who think in structurally different ways should reason about their political beliefs and affiliations differently. Therefore, given a knowledge of the structure of an individual's thought it should be possible to predict the nature of their ideological self-description and the degree of their identification with a political party as measured by standard survey questions.

Method

Subjects. The subject population consisted of twenty-six adults. All of the subjects lived in the New Haven, Connecticut, area, but varied in age, sex, race, income, occupation, and education. They ranged in age from eighteen to seventy-two. Half of the subjects were male; half were female. Three-quarters of the subjects were white; one-quarter were black. The incomes of the subjects ranged between what is received on welfare to $500,000 a year. Some of the subjects were unemployed. The others were employed in a wide variety of occupations (including homemaker, janitor, secretary, salesperson, corporate junior executive, small store manager, lawyer, factory worker). One-third of the subjects had received high school education or less; one-third had some college education; and one-third had two or more years of postgraduate education.

Procedure. Subjects were told they were participating in a study of people's social and political attitudes. Each subject was then asked to do the following (in order of presentation): (1) respond to several closed-ended survey questions; (2) participate in an in-depth interview; and (3) solve two cognitive tasks. Each subject was tested individually by either the author or a research assistant in three one-hour sessions.

The in-depth interview and the cognitive tasks are assessment instruments. They require the subject to make a large number of related assertions and, therefore, allow for a determination of the structure of the subject's thought. Using the definition of types of reasoning as a guide, each of these assessment instruments was analyzed to determine how a subject of each type would respond. Thus, three categories of response—sequential, linear, and systematic—were specified for each instrument. Subjects' performances were then coded accordingly. Coding was done by two raters who were blind both to each other's ratings and to the subject's identity. Rating of the subjects' performances yielded identical scores in seventy-one of seventy-eight cases (three tasks for each of twenty-six subjects). The remaining seven cases were successfully adjudicated.

On the basis of the foregoing assessment, predictions were made regarding each subject's performance on the remaining task. Again, the definition of the types of reasoning was used to analyze how subjects of each type would respond to the survey questions. Predictions were then made accordingly. All of the tasks and the manner in which responses were coded are described in the following paragraphs.

The cognitive tasks. Each subject participated in two Piagetian experiments (Inhelder and Piaget, 1958). Both experiments presented subjects with a problem and gave them the opportunity to solve it. Subjects' activities and remarks were recorded in writing by the interviewer.

In the first experiment subjects were asked to determine what agents combine to create a chemical reaction. First, subjects were shown that a clear liquid turns yellow when several drops of a clear agent were added. They were told that the initially clear liquid came from one or more of four beakers of clear and odorless liquids. They were then given the opportunity to experiment with the four liquids in order to determine the contribution of each to the production of a yellow color. Subjects' performances on the task were classified in the following manner:

Sequential: Sequential thinkers merely track phenomena. They are unable to think causally. All they can do is follow the instruction to apply drops to the clear liquid. Generally, they will try each of the four liquids and stop, saying (despite the evidence of the earlier demonstration) that they cannot make yellow. When prodded, they may attempt one or two combinations of liquids.

Linear: Relating actions, linear thinkers do think causally. They test single liquids and combinations of two liquids until they discover the combination that works. However, when asked to discover the role of the two liquids which do not create yellow, they flounder.

Systematic: Systematic thinkers can juxtapose relations. Consequently, not only can they work their way through the various combinations of liquids to discover the one that creates yellow, they can also determine the role of the remaining two agents. By examining the effect of the remaining agents on the combination of agents which creates yellow, they can determine whether the remaining agents have a neutralizing or neutral effect on the chemical reaction.

In the second experiment subjects observed a swinging pendulum. They were asked to determine what influenced the rate of oscillation. They were told that four factors might be relevant: the length of the string, the weight of the swinging object, the force with which the object is initially pushed, and the height from which it is initially dropped. To discover the answer subjects were encouraged to actually experiment with the pendulum using additional strings of varying length and additional objects of varying weight. Subjects' performances on this second task were classified as follows:

Sequential: Sequential thinkers do not analyze causes or perceive dimensions among actions. Thus, they randomly vary one factor (e.g., weight) and then another. They often vary several at once. Being unable to relate actions, they also have great difficulty determining what oscillation is. They tend to confuse rate of oscillation with the speed with which the swinging object moves.

Linear: Linear thinkers are able to relate actions. Consequently, they are able to understand oscillation and can detect changes in the rate of oscillation. Tending to associate a single cause with an effect and not considering several causes simultaneously, they will tend to inadvertently vary two factors at once.

Systematic: Systematic thinkers see a system of possibly interrelated factors. The problem for them is not to determine which of these has an effect, but to eliminate those which do not. By juxtaposing factors, they can hold several constant in order to vary only one and determine its effect.

The interview. Each subject was interviewed at length about American relations with Iran. The subject was asked to explain what was occurring and why. The meanings of the descriptions and explanations offered were then explored. Throughout the interview the subject was asked to explain the assertions he or she made and to clarify why events transpired in the manner he or she suggested. All of the interviews were taped and later transcribed. Responses were coded as follows:

Sequential: Sequential thinkers are concerned with only present phenomena. While they had heard of Iran and the hostage situation, they did not understand what was happening. They knew a few isolated facts, but did not know how they fit together.

Linear: Linear thinkers can think of groups and consider reports of their action. Thinking in terms of cause and effect, they can map out sequences of exchanges between Iran and the United States. They tend to personalize the exchanges.

Systematic: Systematic thinkers view the interaction between Iran and the United States in the context of the network of interactions which characterize the international system. They also understand that each country's action is not only a response to the acts of other countries, but a response to internal political pressures.

The survey questions. The survey questions were used to measure the degree of respondent's identification with a political party and the degree to which he or she described his or her political thinking in ideological terms. The questions were drawn from the 1980 National Election Study. The questions were read aloud, and the subject's responses were recorded by the interviewer.

To tap party identification the questions used were (1) On this scale from one to seven, where one means "not very strongly" and seven means "very strongly," please choose the number that describes how strongly you support the Republican/Democratic party. (2) Generally speaking, do you usually think of yourself as a Republican, a Democrat, an independent, or what? Would you call yourself a strong Republican/Democrat or a not very strong Republican/Democrat? The party identification questions were combined to create a scale ranging from one (not identified with a party, or independent) to four (very strongly identified with either the Republican or Democratic party).

To measure ideological self-definition the question used was: On this scale from one to seven where one means "extremely liberal" and seven means "extremely conservative," where would you place your political views? Our interest was in the degree of ideological self-definition. Therefore, responses were recoded from one (neutral or no ideological self-definition) to four (extreme ideological self-definition in either a liberal or conservative direction).

Results

Hypothesis 1: Different individuals think in fundamentally different ways. These differences are structural. Therefore, even when confronted with the same simple, clearly defined problem, different individuals may think about that problem in fundamentally different ways. That is, they may think about the task in sequential, linear, or systematic fashion.

To test this hypothesis subjects were asked to solve the chemicals task described earlier. Subjects' performances were categorized by two raters in a double-blind fashion. Scores were identical on twenty-five of the twenty-six cases. The score of the remaining case was successfully adjudicated.

The results indicated that six subjects performed at the sequential level, thirteen subjects performed at the linear level, and seven subjects performed at the systematic level.

In sum, the data provide strong confirmation for the hypothesis that different adults will perform the same task in structurally different ways.

Hypothesis 2: Given the subjectively structured nature of his or her thought, the same individual will think about very different things in the same structurally determined manner. Therefore, the individual's political reasoning should reflect the same structural qualities as that individual's reasoning about other kinds of phenomena.

To test this hypothesis, we examined how each subject performed on two different cognitive tasks (the pendulum task and the chemicals task) and in the interview on American relations with Iran. The responses of twenty-six subjects were again coded in double-blind fashion. Identical scorings were made on seventy-one of the seventy-eight scores. The remaining seven scores were adjudicated.

The results indicated that twenty-one of the twenty-six subjects performed at the same level on all three tasks. Four of the remaining subjects performed at the same level on two of the tasks and at an adjacent level on the third. In all four of these cases the odd performance was quite close to the level of the performance on the other two. None of the subjects performed at three levels or at two levels apart (i.e., one sequential score and one systematic score).

In sum, the hypothesis that an adult performs a number of different tasks at the same structurally determined level is strongly supported by the data.

Hypothesis 3: Individuals who think in structurally different ways think about groups and politics differently. Therefore, structure of thought should differentiate among subjects' political party identifications and ideological self-definition as measured by standard survey questions.

To test this hypothesis, we gave subjects the questions on ideological self-definition and party identification described earlier. Having assessed the subjects' type of thinking, we predicted how they would respond to these questions.

The predictions for subjects' responses to the party identification questions were as follows: Sequential thinkers do not have a self-image, a sense of groups, or an understanding of politics. Therefore, they should evidence low party identification. Linear thinkers have a self-image which is in part determined by group identification, they have a sense of groups, and they have a group-mediated interest in politics. Therefore, linear thinkers should have a high degree of party identification. Systematic thinkers have a self-image. However, they see themselves as the network or system of actions they perform. Thus, their identity is not defined in group-related terms. Therefore, although they may be interested and active in politics, they will not identify with political parties.

The predictions for subjects' responses to the ideological self-definition question were as follows. Sequential thinkers are not oriented to self-definition or to intangibles such as beliefs. Consequently, they should evidence little ideological self-definition. Linear thinkers are oriented to self-definition, and they understand beliefs. However, they see beliefs as causes to action and do not relate them to each other. Therefore, they should also evidence a low level of ideological self-definition. Systematic thinkers are oriented to self-definition and are concerned with the systemic interrelationships among beliefs. Therefore, they should evidence a high degree of ideological self-definition.

The predictions and results are presented in table 1. For both items the variance in the subjects' responses is analyzed by the structure of their thinking. In the case of ideological self-definition the subjects do define themselves differently (the difference is significant at the .03 level) and in the manner predicted. In the case of party identification, differences again occur in the expected direction, but not at a significant level ($p = .10$). However, in light of the small number of cases (21) and the interpretive difficulties associated with the use of closed-ended questions, this result remains encouraging.

Table 1   Political Party Identification
and Ideology by Cognitive Type

Degree of party identification

Cognitive type	Predicted degree of party id	Mean score[a]	Anova	
			F	p
Sequential	Low	2.37	2.60	.10
Linear	High	3.28		
Systematic	Low	1.22		

Degree of ideological self-description

Cognitive type	Predicted degree of ideology	Mean score[b]	Anova	
			F	p
Sequential	Low	2.00	4.25	.03
Linear	Low	2.00		
Systematic	High	3.20		

Note. Number of subjects = 21.

a. Scores range from 1 (not identified/independent) to 4 (strongly identified).

b. Scores range from 1 (neutral self-description) to 4 (very ideological self-description).

Conclusions

We have presented an alternative approach to the study of political thinking. This alternative, the structural developmental approach, is based on three basic assumptions regarding the nature of thinking: (1) thinking is a subjectively structured activity; (2) through interaction with the environment, the structure of an individual's thought develops; and (3) as a result of (1) and (2) different individuals may think in fundamentally different ways. Following on these assumptions are certain conceptual and methodological guidelines for research on political thinking. First, specifically political thinking must be regarded as a determined aspect of thinking more generally. Thus, political thought must be characterized in terms of its underlying cognitive structure. Second, differences in how individuals think about politics have to be identified. These differences must first be described in terms of a developmental hierarchy of cognitive structures, and then explained with reference to variations in the kinds of environments to which individuals are exposed. Third, empirical research must focus on individual subjects and interpret each subject's attitudes in light of the underlying structure of his or her thought.

Adopting this structural developmental approach, we defined three types of political thought and conducted empirical research on a small group of subjects drawn from the New Haven area. The results of our empirical investigation lend strong support to our claims that (1) an individual's thought consists of a structured whole, (2) political thinking is a determined aspect of that whole, and (3) different individuals may think about politics in fundamentally different ways. Furthermore, the results suggest that these structural differences in thinking are captured by our threefold typology of sequential, linear, and systematic thought. These results are drawn from an analysis of subjects' performances on both open-ended tasks required for structural analysis and closed-ended survey items normally used by political scientists.

The theoretical position being advanced here is novel, and the empirical results are surprising. This can easily lead to certain misunderstandings regarding the structural developmental perspective being advanced. To clarify matters, we will address those misunderstandings which arise most frequently. These include (1) the structural developmental typology of political thinking merely constitutes another way of saying some people are smarter than others; (2) even if the typology is meaningful, the hierarchy it defines is merely a reflection of the cultural and personal biases of the investigator; (3) the empirical results—that some people perform differently from others—is an artifact of the methods used (some respondents were relatively unfamiliar with the kinds of tasks presented and, therefore, performed less well); and (4) even if the results are not a methodological artifact, they do no more than suggest that there are differences between rich and poor or educated and uneducated. We will briefly address each of these misunderstandings in turn.

First, there is the misunderstanding regarding the value of conceptualizing political thinking in the manner suggested by our typology. The structural developmental conception does far more than suggest that some people are smarter or more sophisticated than others. On one hand, if one insists on the language of "bright" and "foolish," the typology provides meaning for those words. In normal language use, terms such as bright, sophisticated, or intelligent have little specific meaning. Thus, the definition of sequential, linear, and systematic thought provide greater clarity and specification to a layperson's terminology, which is quite ambiguous. On the other hand, the common meaning of being bright or sophisticated does not suggest that an individual will exhibit these qualities equally in all domains. Rather, these terms are generally used to describe an individual's response to a particular situation or problem. In this regard our structural developmental conception is quite different. It suggests that an individual's thought is structured such that the individual will reason about a wide variety of subject matter in the same way. In other words, it suggests that a bright individual will be bright in precisely the same way regardless of whether that individual is trying to make sense of foreign relations, another person, or a chemistry problem.

Second is the suggestion that, even if the typology meaningfully discriminates between forms of political thinking, it establishes a hierarchy which does no more than reflect and reify the cultural and personal biases of the investigator. Raising a more profound point than the first, this second criticism properly deserves essay-length attention. Given present space limitations, two points are worth making. First and more limited, one would have to be willing to adopt a rather radical epistemological and metaphysical position in order to argue that the development of such abilities as identifying multiple causes or considering an event in a broad spatial and temporal context does not represent an improvement in one's capacity to reason. Second, even if one did adopt a position which turned the hierarchy of types of political thought on its head, the distinction between the types nonetheless could be retained and the central claims being made (that thought is structured and that there are differences between individuals) would remain unchallenged.

Third is the methodological criticism that the results are an artifact; that the differences between individuals observed do not reflect differences in inherent ability, but rather differences in their familiarity with the tasks they were asked to perform. Specifically, the claim here is that college-educated subjects would do better than uneducated subjects because they are more familiar with analytical questions and tasks such as the chemicals task. The criticism is a reasonable one, and two points are worth making. First, even if correct, it is unlikely that the disadvantage of the uneducated subject would be evidenced equally in an open-ended interview, in the performance of a chemistry experiment, and in answering short questions regarding their political beliefs and party affiliations. Second, taking this line of criticism seriously, we did additional research. To test whether poor performance was the result of unfamiliarity with the test materials, we administered the chemicals task to twenty-five sophomore science majors at a major California university. All of the subjects had considerable and comparable exposure to tasks similar to the chemicals task. Nonetheless, only 40 percent of the students performed the task in a manner which reflected systematic thought. Thus, we have both argument and evidence to suggest that the differences between individuals observed cannot be explained in terms of differences in their familiarity with the test materials.

Fourth is the suggestion that the results merely reflect differences in the cultural and educational backgrounds of the subjects. This criticism raises some interesting issues which can be addressed only partially by the evidence collected thus far. First is the issue of the relationship, if any, between type of thought and any demographic variables. Unfortunately, the subject population used in the project reported here was too small to allow for analysis of this type. However, preliminary indications are that while some relationship exists between indicators of power and opportunity (e.g., income and education), it is highly imperfect. The evidence indicates that some relation does exist between sociological variables (e.g., class or level of education) and structure of political thought. At the same time the research provides many examples of people with similar backgrounds who think in fundamentally different ways. Thus, the evidence suggests that such broad sociological categories as class, income, or level of education offer distinctions among environments which are too crude for our purposes. In any case further research must be conducted before the question regarding the demographic correlates of structure of political thinking can be answered. Second, it should be noted that even if individual differences in the structure of political thinking could be accounted for by educational and cultural influences, the typology we offer would still be of great use. On the one hand, it would offer clear specification of the cognitive consequences of such social realities as differences in class and educational background. In this vein, if we were to discover that sequential and linear thought were associated with the powerlessness of the poor, it might assist in our understanding and decoding of the "culture of poverty." On the other hand, it would contribute to our understanding of why the effects of such social realities are so difficult to reverse. As suggested by both structural developmental theory and data, cognitive structure powerfully defines the environment to which the individual is exposed and, therefore, is not easily transformed.

Despite the adequacy of our response to the aforementioned criticisms, it is certainly the case that the analysis reported here is only a first step in the development and application of this structural developmental approach. At a theoretical level the definition of the types of political thinking must be further elaborated. How thinkers of each type understand such phenomena as political actors, power, causes of action, and political systems must be further specified. At the same time an attempt must be made to define environments in a cognitively relevant manner. Then, a theory of the impact of environments on the structure of political thinking may be formulated. Such a theory might address the temporary as well as the long-term effects of environments on political thinking. At an empirical level a great deal more work must be done to determine the adequacy of the typology of sequential, linear, and systematic political thought. New materials must be used to address different aspects of the subjects' political reasoning. This must be complemented by an attempt to empirically establish the relationship between political environments and types of political thought.

A Piagetian Developmental Theory
of Political Institutions

Given their developmental focus and their associations with cognitive adequacy, Piagetian theories would appear directly applicable to the study of macro-level political development. Indeed, a variety of theorists already conjecture, argue, or assume that political development is rooted in some form of cognitive development.[1]

To make the connection is trickier than it might appear, however, since both of the obvious ways of applying Piagetian theories are flawed. The first is to view societies as developing organisms, thus subject to the universal Piagetian functions of organization and adaptation. Unfortunately, such an approach fails on several counts. First, it commits the "organismic fallacy" by asserting without proof that societies behave as organisms. Second, the development of a social organism does not square particularly well with the normative connotations of development. Intuitively, a more developed society is one in which people are able to maintain more ethically grounded relations with one another. However "ethically grounded" is defined, it seems to relate to the interactions of individuals, not to the hypothesized developmental needs of a reified "social organism." Third, such an approach reifies what is merely a human creation. "Society" refers to different constructions at different times and places. The nation-state currently appears to be the dominant referent of "society," but family, clan, fief, village, caste, religion, profession, and corporation also have been, are now, or may yet be the dominant referents of the term. To say that "a society" develops is to place too much weight on what is a human, and thus only a contingent, construction. Finally, if theorists attempt to avoid this difficulty by positing the entire world as the society in question, the Piagetian approach breaks down for lack of an external environment with which such an organism could interact. For all of these reasons, regarding society as an organism in an attempt to apply Piagetian methods seems pretty clearly to be a dead end.

The second obvious way to apply Piagetian developmental psychology to political development is by aggregation: defining a society as developed in proportion to the average level of its members' development. Such an approach commits the composition fallacy, however, by assuming that a society is no more than the aggregate of its members. Such aggregation is clearly not consonant with our sense of political development: we would never consider a society developed in which a small, powerful, venal oligarchy enslaved a populace of philosopher-saints.

Despite its problems, the "aggregation" approach seems more promising than the "social organism" approach. Even if aggregates have emergent properties beyond those of their constituent parts, there is some plausibility to the notion that an aggregation of cognitively developed individuals has a greater capability of creating a developed society than an aggregation of less-developed individuals. Even though direct aggregation has theoretical flaws, there may be a more subtle connection by which the plausibility of the approach can be upheld.

This chapter presents a means of doing so: of showing how genetic epistemology may be applied to political development (to political development specifically, but also, by extension, to other concepts pertaining to social aggregates). Two issues have to be dealt with: first, we must define the nature of the individual development most appropriate for extension to political development; and second, we must describe the exact relationship between this micro-level and its associated macro-level development.

The first issue can be settled by reflecting on the implicit normative claims of the term "political development." Without normative grounding, development becomes merely change, a much looser term. If for no other reason than linguistic accuracy, admissible conceptualizations of political development must solve the problem of normative grounding.[2]

More is at stake than linguistics, however. In fact, even "value-neutral" theories of social change require normative grounding, because social action implicitly requires normative choice. Regardless of the apparent constraints on their actions, social actors "always already" choose how to relate to one another. The theory of such choice is a normative theory (Kohlberg, 1981a; Habermas, 1983; Chilton, 1989). Thus, Huntington's (1971) suggestion—that social science turn from "development" to "change"—is based on an illusion. Theories of change offer only the dubious advantage of better disguising our normative ground.

The second issue, of the relationship between micro-level and macro-level development, really involves three related issues: establishing the locus of development; solving the micro-macro relationship problem; and laying out the consequences of the micro-macro relationship for developmental dynamics. First, what is it that develops in political development: what is the locus of development? Any theory of political development must point to something measurable as development: operationalization cannot substitute for conceptualization. For example, an index combining McDonald's per capita sales and average life-span might reflect a development process, but it does not advance our theoretical grasp of that process. Theories of development have to conceptualize what it is that develops. That conceptualization may be impossible to measure in practice, but it must be at least ideally operationalizable. Without a definite locus of development, any empirical results are left suspended in mid-air.

Current theories differ over this locus of development, the major alternative loci being individuals and institutions. Theorists who point to the individual as the locus (e.g., Hagen, 1962; McClelland, 1976; Almond and Verba, 1963) see aggregated developmental shifts of individuals as constituting overall political development. Theorists who point to institutions as the locus (e.g., LaPalombara, 1967; Pye, 1966) see development in the rise of institutional frameworks, to which people adapt willy-nilly. Inasmuch as these theorists define, in potentially operationalizable form, that which develops, their theories do solve this theoretical problem.

Not all theories solve this problem, however. Hegel's (1975) philosophy of history points to "The Spirit" or "The Idea" as the locus of development, but this concept seems imprecise and unmeasurable. Eckstein (1982) defines the locus of political development as "politics itself," but he does not clarify that rather circular definition. In the absence of theoretical elaboration these theories do not solve the locus of development problem and so are inadmissible.

If the locus of development problem were not difficult enough, development theorists also face the problem of the micro-macro connection. Wherever they locate development, admissible conceptualizations cannot neglect development's implications for both individuals and institutions. Individual development alone is not a sufficient condition for development, because individual virtue does not imply the presence of developed institutional structure. But neither is institutional structure alone sufficient for development. With Vietnam a case in point, we would never consider a society developed in which "developed" institutions were imposed on people for whom they had no meaning. Even if the populace were grudgingly willing (and able) to operate and maintain such institutions, the general morality of forcing such grudging acquiescence is questionable. If there is such a thing as development, then, it clearly must refer to both individuals and institutions and to the ways in which the two are connected. Institutions do not inevitably create compliant individuals, and developed individuals are not necessarily able to create appropriate institutions. Although interdependent, individuals and institutions are in no sense identical. Thus, conceptions of development must depict how development results in both different individuals and different institutions.

Last, what trajectory and dynamics do social development have? These are fairly well understood for individual development, but to what extent or in what ways are their micro-level forms carried over to macro-level development? To what degree is macro-level development subject to the same forces as micro-level development?

The remainder of this chapter deals with these questions. We advance a Piagetian reconceptualization of political culture, which is then used to define political development. We also present the cultural and institutional concomitants of political development, flesh out the concept through historical examples, and argue that the concept solves the locus of development and micro-macro connection problems. Then we explore the forces affecting the trajectory and dynamics of political development. Finally, we review the role that genetic epistemology has played in the discussion, arguing that it is both necessary and sufficient for an adequate conception of political development.

Political Culture and Cognitive Structure

Three Systems: Individual, Cultural, and Social

We begin by distinguishing three aspects of society: the individual system, the cultural system, and the social system.[3] The individual system consists of variables describing a person that do not logically depend on characteristics of other people. One actor's characteristics may be empirically related to another's (e.g., spouses tend to share values), but they are not related of necessity (e.g., it is conceivable that one spouse but not the other believes democracy is good). Thus, beliefs, attitudes, values (Almond, 1956), and assumptions (Elkins and Simeon, 1979) are located in the individual system, but roles and other social positions are not. A belief in democracy can be held independently of others' beliefs or characteristics, but the role of a ruler exists only vis-à-vis the counterpart role of subject.

The cultural and social systems are distinguished from the individual system in that they possess emergent properties, that is, properties that cannot be derived from the characteristics of individuals considered in isolation. Lehman (1972) defines "cultural items . . . as essentially *supramembership* in nature so that their analytical status does not flow directly from the properties of individual actors" (p. 362).

Aggregations of individual properties are also part of the individual system, despite current research that views them as "cultural." These aggregate properties may point to or indicate cultural properties, as Lehman (1971) grants, but they are not cultural properties themselves, having no supramembership quality. Almond's and Verba's (1963) definition of political culture—"the particular distribution of patterns of orientation toward political objects among the members of the nation" (pp. 12–13)—applies to the individual system, not the cultural system.[4] As Lehman (1972) notes, the individual-system definition of political culture "is convenient for those [using] the survey method, but it suffers from allowing one's methodological preference to define one's theoretical formulation" (p. 362).

Individual-system definitions create difficulty by leading researchers inevitably away from important avenues of analysis. The absence of such important avenues can be seen in David McClelland's (1976) work on the achieving society. McClelland establishes a relationship only between two individual system variables—need for achievement and economic output—and shows that this relationship obtains at both the individual and aggregate level. However, he does not discuss whether different aggregate levels of need for achievement might produce different *cultural* forms. Perhaps low need for achievement produces a feudal economy structure, and high need for achievement produces a market economy structure. McClelland's work remains at the individual level and thus constitutes merely a "busy beaver" theory of growth: lots of achievers produce lots of achievements. By concentrating on individual characteristics, researchers penalize themselves doubly: they neglect culture's supramembership effects, which might assist them to explain some aspects of their aggregate data, or, even worse, they study phenomena irrelevant to their real purpose (e.g., culture rather than the aggregate individual seems the most appropriate focus for both Almond and Verba, 1963, and McClelland, 1976).

The Cultural System

The cultural system of any collectivity is all publicly common ways of relating in that collectivity.[5] There are four distinguishing features of this definition: the focus on "relating," the focus on "ways" of relating, the requirement that these ways of relating be "common," and the further requirement that they be "publicly" common. We address each of these features in turn.

The first feature of culture is that it concerns relationships, not individuals in isolation. For example, one aspect of the political cultural system is the courtesy system. If a person steps on my foot in the subway, I say "excuse me" rather than some abusive alternative: the courtesy system tells me how I am to relate to the clumsy people in my life. It is a way of *relating* to people. Political culture cannot be located in the individual system, because a relationship cannot be a characteristic of an individual in isolation. Previous definitions of political culture have tended to lose sight of the fact that institutional arrangements are formed by relationships, not isolated actors.

How we relate to one another is both the general subject of empirical social science (how *do* we relate to one another) and the central concern of normative social theory (how *should* we relate to one another). We are thus fascinated by Geertz's (1973) description of the Balinese cockfight in the context of Balinese village life only incidentally because it describes strange and interesting practices, but more importantly because it reveals how the Balinese relate to one another. The cockfights do not just *symbolize* how the Balinese relate—they *are* a way they relate. If Geertz had simply viewed the cockfight as a symbol of Balinese life, or had described the Balinese "beliefs, attitudes, and values" concerning the cockfight, he would have led his readers away from the cockfight's immediate significance as a way the Balinese relate to one another. It is the description of this way of relating *as* a way of relating that makes it of such theoretical interest and, not by accident, human interest.

The second feature of political culture is that it concerns "ways" of relating. Culture does not consist of fragmented patterns of behavior, but of self-consistent systems of relating. The systems may be integrated to a greater or lesser extent, but they are systems, not sets of unrelated elements. This cohesiveness has been recognized in many definitions of political culture. Almond and Verba (1963) follow Parsons when they refer to "patterns of orientation," this term connoting an integrated system and recalling Parsons's "pattern variables." Elazar's (1966) three "political subcultures" are each discussed as a unified orientation. Dittmer (1977) defines political culture as a "symbol system." All call attention to culture's interdependent unity.

The third feature of political culture is that the ways of relating are "common," that is, known to all participants in the culture. Commonality is of course a major concern of current political culture research: the identification of beliefs, attitudes, and values that are common within the society.[6] Certainly if a collectivity is to possess a political culture, its members must share a common way of relating.

Though commonality is important to culture, it does not define culture, because there are potentially many common ways to relate to other people. This ambiguity of commonness is revealed in that experiment (Garfinkel, 1967) in which a college student goes home for a visit and baffles his family by acting like a guest rather than a family member. The ambiguity arises because both "guest" and "family member" are ways of relating that are potentially applicable to the situation and known to the family members. The variability of ways of relating can also be seen even in the span of one's own life, both in time (contrast children's to adults' ways of relating) and space (contrast one's ways of relating with one's spouse to those with one's Senator).[7]

The fourth feature of political culture, therefore, is the elimination of relational ambiguity by focusing on the "publicly" common way of relating. The cultural system is unique because it is publicly regarded as the standard or norm of relating. Culture is not just *a* way of relating to others—it is *the* way in which, without prior negotiations, people expect to deal with others in the given context. Although no single culture may apply to all interactions, cues surrounding each interaction enable the individual to choose the appropriate way of relating.[8] The nature and operation of these cues is a central concern of symbolic interactionism (see Hewitt, 1979, chapter 4).

In most situations there is an implicit culture. This gives Garfinkel's experiment its impact: the student's behavior is potentially appropriate, but it causes confusion nevertheless because it does not conform to the existing implicit culture. Schelling (1980, chapter 3) specifically points out the importance of a mutually understood context of behavior in the strategy of conflict. Political culture provides—indeed, is—such a context.

The emphasis on public commonness is necessary for four important theoretical reasons. First, it eliminates ad hoc specifications of a culture. We loosely term the United States a culture, but what criterion beyond our own judgment shows that it is? *The Civic Culture* (Almond and Verba, 1963) finds quite disparate views in the United States; but by what right do we assume this diversity to be one culture? Theorists offer justifications that are only truculent ("Because I say it's a culture"), tautological ("Because it's all the United States"), or problematic ("Because it has one government"). The public commonness restriction insists that a culture extends only so far as people choose the same way to relate to one another, which seems to be what people mean when they refer to a group as a culture.

The concept of public commonness—the actual *use* of a way of relating—makes us more aware of who does and who does not "participate in the culture." Even in such a highly selective and self-conscious institution as Congress, for example, certain members exhibit inappropriate behavior. We must differentiate Congress's strategic advantages, shared by all 535 members, from Congress's dominant culture, which may be shared by only 534, or 533, etc. Nothing guarantees that any given agglomeration of people will have a culture.

Second, the public commonness restriction allows cultures to be studied and characterized as wholes, because by definition all actors in the culture work within shared, and acted-upon, ways of relating. The analyst can reintroduce the natural complexity of a mixed society through concepts of subculture and cultural conflict, while allowing analytic power to be applied to truly homogeneous cultures.

Third, the insistence upon publicness distinguishes acquiescence from approval by acknowledging that cultural expectations can differ from individuals' preferred ways of relating. This distinction frees our conceptualization of political culture from Talcott Parsons's much-criticized insistence on value consensus. "When in

Rome, do as the Romans do" could be the official motto of political culture: one might like to deal with people in a certain way, but prior, publicly common expectations constrain one's behavior. The existence of a political culture is not determined by all people's subscribing to the culture, liking it, or regarding it as legitimate. Rather, it is determined by the ways of relating that people actually use to coordinate their dealings with one another. Individual preferences obviously limit the variety of ways of relating that can become publicly common, but individual preference and public commonness are logically distinct. Culture is what is publicly expected, not what is individually preferred.

Fourth, considerations of public commonness underlie two important social phenomena: socialization and cultural change. Public commonness is difficult to maintain, and so is responsible for society's immense investment of labor in schooling and other socialization. Public commonness is also difficult to establish and alter. Immense social upheavals are required for cultural change, perhaps not initially while new ways of relating become common, but certainly later while they become publicly common. Researchers can understand fully neither socialization nor social change without adducing the concept of public commonness.

The Linkage of Individual, Cultural, and Social Systems

The individual system is linked to the cultural system through people's beliefs about what the publicly common ways of relating are. On one hand, such beliefs are part of the individual system because they are held by individuals. On the other hand, such beliefs are part of the cultural system because, to the extent that they are in fact shared, they are the actual expression of the cultural system.

Researchers can thus examine these beliefs from the perspective of either system. As part of the individual system these beliefs are like any others. Researchers can examine their intrapsychic origins and dynamics, their variation within the population, and so on. These are the concerns of Kemeny-type symbolic interactionism, which explores conflicts of individual beliefs about the operant cultural system (Kemeny, 1976).

As part of the cultural system, these beliefs stem from and express a common cultural system, not individual idiosyncrasies. Researchers can examine the origins of the beliefs in socialization and hegemonic control of the culture, the internal structure of the beliefs (e.g., as role systems), and so on. These are the concerns of role theory and of Hewitt-type symbolic interactionism, which explores the nature of, and the cues eliciting usage of, the operant cultural system (Hewitt, 1979).

One especially important link between the individual and cultural systems is the normative evaluations of a culture. On one hand, the evaluations are part of the individual system: one person's evaluation does not depend of necessity upon another person's. On the other hand, shared evaluations that are known to be shared are part of the cultural system.

If the evaluations are negative, this can result in a cultural change (or a "deviant" culture). For example, if the population at large becomes convinced that the tax system is unfair, then an underground economy can spring up to avoid the system. However, shared negative evaluations do not by themselves constitute a culture. Rejection of one cultural system does not mean creation of a new one: as politicians say, "You can't beat somebody with nobody." Shared knowledge that many people reject the existing culture may encourage a search for a counter-culture, but it does not produce one. For example, some people observe the increasing proportion of "independent" voters and call for an Independent Party. But "independent" voters are not all of a kind: they include the ignorant, the passive, libertarians, anarcho-syndicalists, and so on. Mere shared negative valence does not produce a culture.

We must still distinguish the social and cultural systems. Although both systems consist of emergent properties, Parsons (1961) specifically notes that the two systems must be distinguished:

> One aspect [of the delineation of the place of social systems within the frame of reference of action], that of the distinction between the *analytically* defined "individual" and the systems

generated by the process of social interaction [that is, between the individual system on the one hand and the cultural and social systems on the other], can be taken for granted. But this is not enough for our purposes, primarily because it fails to make another analytically crucial distinction, namely, that between social systems and cultural systems. . . . The clear need for [this] distinction has only gradually been emerging in sociology and anthropology. (p. 33)

The cultural and social systems differ in that the cultural system has normative significance (understood in Habermas's, 1979a, "performative mode"), and the social system has objective patterns of interaction (understood in Habermas's, 1979a, "objective mode"). The cultural system is directive, and its prescriptions are subject to moral evaluation; the social system is descriptive, and its descriptions are subject to scientific evaluation. The social system can acquire, but never contains, human meaning as a normatively significant, publicly common way of relating. The cultural system can generate—but is not itself—regular patterns of social interaction.

Although the cultural and social systems are distinguished, they are also linked. Just as individual beliefs about the cultural system link the individual and cultural systems, so do institutions link the cultural and social systems. On one hand, institutions are part of the cultural system because they embody publicly common ways of relating. On the other hand, institutions are part of the social system because they empirically evidence regular patterns of interaction.

Researchers can thus examine institutions from the perspective of either system. As part of the cultural system, institutions can be studied phenomenologically to determine what publicly common, normative expectations about relationships they represent. The analytical-theoretical focus is therefore on the nature of these expectations and only secondarily on the resulting behavior. This perspective is adopted by Fenno (1978) and Kingdon (1973), who describe in phenomenological terms how members of Congress relate to their constituents (Fenno) and to other members (Kingdon).

As part of the social system, institutions can be studied empirically to determine their regular patterns of interaction. The analytical-theoretical focus is therefore on what regularities of behavior can be detected, and only secondarily on what normative expectations underlie them. This perspective is adopted by Chilton (1977) and White et al. (1975), who attempt to describe the empirical relationships within various collectivities. For example, White et al. analyzed Sampson's (1978) monastery data and discovered an objective sociometric pattern of three groups. Two of these were mutually exclusive: with virtually no exceptions, members had feelings of liking and esteem for their own group's members and feelings of antagonism and disesteem for the other group's members.[9] White's "block-modeling" approach reduces the sociomatrices to three basic elements: a set of roles (e.g., for the monastery, the roles "Loyal Opposition member" and "Young Turks member"); role assignments for the actors (e.g., the assignment of each monk to one of the two groups); and role interaction patterns (e.g., a 2 x 2 role interaction matrix showing that positive relations lie within, and not between, the two groups). This role interpretation employs cultural system language, but nevertheless it remains part of the social system: it characterizes objective patterns of interaction, not necessarily any shared subjective interpretations producing those patterns.

White's approach attempts, often successfully, to deduce a society's culture from its social structure. Nevertheless, analysts must recognize the problematic nature of that deduction, because not all regular patterns of interaction stem from the cultural system. For example, one might observe a collection of people around a water cooler at 10:42 A.M. each day. If this collection were maintained solely by 10:42 thirst and not by a desire to interact, then this regular pattern of interaction would not be considered part of the cultural system. As White et al. (1975) state it, "social structure is regularities in the patterns of relations among concrete entities; it is *not* a harmony among abstract norms and values" (p. 733).

Such regular patterns can, however, become part of the cultural system simply by being recognized and desired as a point of cultural orientation—a way of creating meaning out of the jumble of life. In New Mexico a group of state politicians are known widely as "The

Mama Lucy Gang" because they attended the same college, where they frequently ate together at a local restaurant called "Mama Lucy's." The term "Mama Lucy Gang" does not refer to their dining preferences or their educational background; rather, it crystallizes and raises to general cultural consciousness a recognition of what they shared and still share. It points to, makes meaningful, and thereby maintains the way they relate to one another. The term creates a cultural object out of a social system regularity.

Inter-system Linkages in Stable and Unstable Societies

In a stable society the individual, cultural, and social systems are tightly linked. The cultural system produces individual characteristics through socialization and the consequent individual recognition of cultural expectations. Individuals reinforce the cultural system by supporting it: by valuing it, or simply by acquiescing to its expectations. The cultural system also produces the social system through the empirical patterns of interaction reflecting cultural norms. The social system reinforces, in turn, the cultural system when people raise common behavioral patterns into aspects of culture. These bidirectional relationships among the cultural, individual, and social systems are why Parsons (1961) speaks of the systems as "interpenetrating" (p. 36). The exact distinction among them therefore becomes less important in stable societies than in unstable societies. Research based on the analysis of any of the three systems yields the same results. The theoretical distinctiveness of the systems does not prohibit their empirical connection.

In an unstable society, on the other hand, social dynamics arise from the interaction of dissimilar systems. The systems still affect one another, but the result in this case is social change. Lehman (1972) points out one such source of change: "New political institutions may generate new doctrines of legitimacy" (p. 367). For example, a group of school-teachers may happen to gather regularly in the faculty lounge during a common free period and may come to identify themselves as a "group" rather than an "accidental meeting." Lehman goes on to say that "doctrines of legitimacy may also promote new institutions" (p. 367, emphasis removed). For example, the cultural legitimacy of smoking has changed, with the consequent institutional development of no-smoking areas in restaurants. Once the initial harmony among them is broken, the three systems must change and respond to change in each other. Consider Everett Hagen's (1962) theory of social change. Hagen postulates that an exogenous social system change produces a change in the cultural system in which one social class suffers "withdrawal of status respect." This cultural system change causes a change in the socialization of the affected class that leads to changes in the personalities of the people of that class, i.e., it leads to changes in the individual system. These changes have other consequences, and so on.

Description of a stable society solely in terms of its individual system may be adequate, but description of an unstable society in those terms cannot be. To the extent that it studies only the individual system, political research is unable to describe social change deriving from cultural and social system factors.

For example, consider the civil rights movement in the United States. The civil rights movement originated in a cultural change: a conscious, collective insistence by black Americans (and others) on a new way of relating. This cultural change led to changes both in the individual system (because, among other things, people had to come to terms with the changes in the culture) and in the social system (because, among other things, civil rights legislation led people to behave differently toward each other).[10] These changes in the social system led in turn to changes in the individual system (say, greater resentment of the federal government). The civil rights movement was not a consequence of any particular change in Americans' beliefs, attitudes, and values concerning institutionalized racism.[11] It resulted in but was not caused by such a change. Research restricted to the individual system can reveal changes in attitudes that resulted from the civil rights movement, as Hyman and Sheatsley (1956) and Sheatsley, Taylor and Greeley (1978) do, but it cannot predict future changes, because the agency of change is outside the research's scope. Thus, the study of political change must start with the cultural system.

The Cognitive Structure of Ways of Relating and Political Culture

The term "ways of relating" has a nice behavioral ring to it, raising images of objective, observable patterns of behavior. Such images must be rejected, however. Social behavior comes not out of fixed behavior patterns but rather out of the exercise of action schemas within the flowing environment. Ways of relating are constituted as people engage social situations by interpreting them. People employ interpretive schemas to identify, interconnect, and consequently make meaningful their own and others' actions. Whether such schemas organize simple actions or complex internalized representations of action, the schemas constitute reasoning. Even ordinary discourse recognizes a reasoning process organizing action: people ask "Why did you do that?" and expect a reason; or alternatively they ask "How did you come to do that?" and expect a coherent description.[12]

Fixed environments may induce recurrent responses, but environmental changes quickly reveal these responses' foundation in reasoning. Bureaucrats, for example, appear to employ regular, mindless bureaucratic procedures. But even obedient clients can present problems calling for interpretation, and some clients, as Danet (1971) points out, also use extralegal appeals: sob stories, bribes, and even threats. Such appeals require the bureaucrat to re-reason his or her rote use of the rulebook. "What is the value of following the rules when set against (e.g.) a monetary gain for myself?" the bureaucrat must ask. The answer may appear obvious to the reader, but the long history of bureaucratic corruption shows it is not always obvious to bureaucrats. In short, any way of relating, including that represented by the most rule-bound bureaucracy, is founded on reasoning rather than fixed rules. Researchers must, therefore, inquire into people's understandings of their behavior—the schemas they employ—rather than their behavior alone.

Reasoning about one's social behavior is ipso facto moral reasoning, because it shows how one takes the claims of others into account—which claims, in what way, and to what extent. When one decides how to behave in relation to others, one is of necessity making a moral judgment. This is not to say all such judgments are of equal moral significance, or require equal deliberation. Clearly, some judgments, such as stepping out of someone's path on a sidewalk, require little thought or effort. The point remains, however, that a decision is made.

An extensive body of longitudinal, cross-cultural, and cross-sectional research has shown that moral reasoning follows a Piagetian developmental sequence of cognitive structures. This sequence of structures has been elaborated most clearly by Lawrence Kohlberg and his colleagues. Kohlberg's research supports the following claims for his sequence of stages:[13]

(1) Moral reasoning varies in its structure (the logical inter-relationships of the concepts) among at least six possible stages.

(2) The stages can be hierarchically ordered such that each stage represents an integration and differentiation of the previous stage (Kohlberg, 1981 and 1984a; Kohlberg, Levine, and Hewer, 1984a).[14]

(3) Stages are acquired in hierarchical order, with no skipping of stages and no retrogression to lower stages (Colby et al., 1983).

(4) Progression through the stages depends initially on the successive recognition of each stage's relativity to different moral concerns and perspectives and, ultimately, on an appropriate reorganization of that stage to embrace and coordinate those perspectives. Thus progression is not inevitable, but it is possible—for any person, at any stage, whenever he or she perceives such relativity (Kohlberg, 1981, 1984a).

(5) The above statements apply uniformly to all cultures. (Kohlberg, 1981; Kohlberg, Levine, and Hewer, 1984a; Nisan and Kohlberg, 1984; Snarey, Reimer, and Kohlberg, 1984; Weinreich, 1977; Edwards, 1975. Dasen, 1977, reviews cross-cultural tests of Piagetian theories in general.)

The research can support these strong claims because it studies the structure of moral reasoning, not the content. Let us examine this distinction more closely. One stage of moral reasoning (called "Stage 3" in Kohlberg's work) involves a "Golden Rule" maintenance of interpersonal relations through mutual role-taking. Consider the following two hypothetical Stage 3 answers to the question of whether a judge should give jail terms to conscientious objectors: (a) "The judge should put them in jail because that's what's expected of judges"; or (b) "The judge should put herself in the conscientious objector's place and have a heart." In both answers the reasoning is structured in terms of the maintenance of good interpersonal relations and mutual role-taking. The conclusions drawn are opposite and the concerns brought to bear are different, of course, but these content differences stem from a very minor difference in thinking. The first answer tells the judge to role-take with other members of society, while the second answer tells her to role-take with the accused. The role-taking perspective is ambiguous in its application, and the diversity of content thus stems from the ambiguity of the simple Stage 3 structure. The distinction between content and structure is especially crucial in cross-cultural work, where content differences are extreme.

For those not familiar with the stage sequence, figure 1 below lists Kohlberg's descriptive title for each stage.[15] Next to each stage we list various forms of interpersonal relations or forms of influence organized at that stage in the United States. For example, "friendship" is commonly understood in U.S. society as a Stage 3 relationship: the rights and obligations of friendship arise from mutual, ideal application of the Golden Rule.

Figure 1 requires two theoretical clarifications. The first has to do with the validity of placing any particular interpersonal relationship at a single stage. Consider "friendship" once again. Even though the term seems most naturally to denote a Stage 3 mutual maintenance of an ideal, reciprocated, positive relationship, other usages are possible. Philosophers and theologians could enrich and elaborate the concept at higher stages: predicating "true" friendship on mutual support of an overarching moral order (Stage 4), as communists call each other "comrade." Even relationships organized at lower stages might be called friendship, as in the following Stage 2 usage: "The girl returned smiling. 'The pilot is *very* susceptible,' she said. 'If he don't like you, he don't take you. But I show him your photograph and he has agreed to *surcharger*. He is allowed to take only thirty-one *personnes* but he take you, he don't care, he do it for friendship if you give him one thousand five hundred riels'" (Le Carré, 1977, p.

Figure 1   Speculative Stage Classifications of Ways of Relating

Kohlberg's descriptive title	Forms of interpersonal relations and influence
1 Punishment and obedience ("might makes right")	Domination; threats; extortion; physical compulsion; seizure by force
2 Individual instrumental purpose and exchange ("What's in it for me?")	Barter and trading; deterrence by revenge; bribery; corvee labor; prebend; curses; feudal fealty and vassalage
3 Mutual interpersonal expectations, relationships, and conformity (the concrete Golden Rule)	Friendship; *compadrazgo*; romantic or courtly love
4 Social system and conscience maintenance ("law and order")	Mutual support of moral system
5 Prior rights and social contract or utility	Mutual respect; rational debate, fair competition, and scientific testing
6 Universal ethical principles (the second-order Golden Rule)	*Satyagraha; agape*; undistorted communicative action; mutual care

358). Thus, relational names can apply to many different relationships. Furthermore, since each stage-specific relationship arises out of actors' earlier understandings of it, no single form of the relationship is inherently the "ideal" form. What figure 1 gives, therefore, is only the cognitive stage at which the relationship seems to be most commonly understood.

A second clarification concerns the cultural specificity of the named forms of relationship/influence. Such specificity violates the earlier claim for the moral stages' cultural universality. Figure 1 associates Kohlberg's culturally universal structural stages with culturally specific examples. However, these examples can, and we hope will, be supplemented by examples from other cultures, e.g., the relationships and influences based on *giri* in Japanese culture (Benedict, 1946). The cultural specificity of the examples is not used later to create a culturally specific theory of development, even while culturally specific examples must inevitably be employed to illustrate the theory.

A Piagetian Theory of Political Development

Political Development Is the Cognitive-Structural Development of Political Culture

If ways of relating (forms of relationship and influence) have the same structures as individual moral reasoning, then each political culture can be placed in a hierarchy corresponding to Kohlberg's six stages. *Political development is the movement of a political culture to organization by a higher cognitive-structural stage.* This definition focuses on changes neither of individuals nor of social systems, but rather of the political culture.

Stages of Institutional Forms in Political Development

In this section our goal is to discover for each stage what institutions can exist when social actors are limited to relationships at that stage. Moral reasoning and its associated forms of relationship and influence focus on how individuals deal with one another, but these relationships can be integrated into certain institutions without demanding additional cognitive complexity on the part of social actors. Figure 2 summarizes the discussion; refer back to figure 1 for the associated stages of moral reasoning.[16]

In this analysis we assume the existence of a culture and so avoid problems of dissent and/or cultural ignorance. The present theory can handle such problems without loss of generality by studying subcultures, meaning those subsets of society that do have a publicly common way of relating. Different subcultures can have different ways of relating, naturally. Different subcultures can also relate

Figure 2   Speculative Stage Classification of Social Forms

Forms of interpersonal relations and influence	Associated social institutions
1 Domination; threats; extortion; physical compulsion; seizure by force	Pecking order; slavery; prison and other total institutions
2 Barter and trading; deterrence by revenge; bribery; corvee labor; prebend; curses; feudal fealty and vassalage	Early feudal system; exchange patronage systems; tax farming; hostages
3 Friendship; *compadrazgo*; romantic or courtly love	Medieval towns; social patronage or client system; late medieval aristocracy; estates (*Staende*); dualistic *Staendestaat*; corporatism
4 Mutual support of moral system	Modern army; bureaucracy; fascism; tyranny of majority rule; absolutism
5 Mutual respect; rational debate, fair competition, and scientific testing	Democracies protecting civil rights and liberties; due process; capitalist market economies; "normal science"
6 *Satyagraha*; *agape*; undistorted communicative action; mutual care	(none currently known)

to one another, as when fraternity members relate within their individual houses as "brothers" and with the members of other houses as "fellow Greeks." The presence of different subcultures creates certain social dynamics (conflict, compromise, development), but dynamics do not concern us here.

Stage 1 possesses few and very simple ways of relating. The institutions built up from these relationships are accordingly very limited, restricted to pecking-order hierarchies and slavery. Even such an "institution" as an extortion racket involves at heart no more than one person threatening another; little organization is involved. The organization emerging from Stage 1 is the result of immediate responses, not of any social vision.

Do any Stage 1 institutions currently exist, and have they existed in the past? Bullying and extortion rackets still exist among children and to some extent among adults, and slavery still exists in isolated areas of the world. Maximum-security prisons may contain a Stage 1 culture. Radding (personal communication) has speculated that Nazism was based on a Stage 1 worship of force.

The social forms built up from Stage 2 relationships are more varied than Stage 1 forms but still operate on the narrow bases of positive exchange (bribery, we call it) and negative exchange (revenge). For example, the Roman, Byzantine, and other empires were organized on the "venal control" or "tax farming" system (Frey, 1971), which relied only on Stage 2 relationships. Governors related to the emperor on a positive exchange basis, giving the emperor both protection from outlying barbarians and an annual tribute levied on the subject population, while receiving both military support and the right to all taxes collected beyond the emperor's tribute. The governor's loyalty was additionally ensured by the negative exchange practice of keeping hostages: the governor's family would remain in the imperial capital or even in the emperor's household and thus could be punished for any misdeeds of the governor.[17] This straightforward Stage 2 relationship between emperor and governor was duplicated at lower levels: between the governor and his subgovernors; between each subgovernor and his district superintendents; between each district superintendent and the district's village headmen; and between each village headman and the heads of the village families. Note that no vision of the total system was required by any of its participants: what appears to be a complex totality is in fact composed simply of hierarchically nested, individual, Stage 2 relationships.

Stage 2 institutions have existed in many areas and eras, not just in empires. The early feudal ages were characterized by Stage 2 organization; feudal lords exchanged protection for rent and service from their vassals.[18] Feuds (though the term apparently does not arise from the same word as feudal), also are based on a Stage 2 relationship of systematic, alternating revenge. Feuds may not ordinarily be considered social institutions, but they certainly represent regularly occurring behavior motivated by a publicly common way of relating, and so accordingly deserve to be termed a "social form." Bloch (1961, chapter 9) discusses the "vendetta," which had some legal/social sanction as late as the thirteenth century. It should be no surprise that Stage 2 feudal society should include such a social form. Currently, political scientists study Stage 2 institutions in terms of "clientelism," a concept applicable to societies worldwide. The research collections of Schmidt et al. (1977) and Eisenstadt and Lemarchand (1981) include studies of clientelism in societies both Western and non-Western, developing and developed, urban and rural. The pervasiveness of clientelism would appear to arise from the simplicity of its underlying cognitive structure.

Although Stage 2 institutions obviously exist around the world, social scientists appear to be preoccupied with them to the point that Stage 3 ties are misread as thin disguises for selfish interests. Lande (1977), for example, writes his theory of dyadic relationships exclusively in Stage 2 terms: "Dyadic relationships, being systems of exchange or barter, must be between individuals who are unalike. . . . [One partner] is not likely to be asked to interest himself in the [other's] trade as a whole. . . . The interests that unite the leader and his followers are particular rather than categorical: the purpose is not the attainment of a common general objective but the advancement of the leader's and his followers' complementary private interests" (pp. 507–508). Hall's (1977) theoretical discussion of the patron-client relationship follows similar lines. Such formulations miss Stage 3 institutional forms (e.g., of patron-client relations), not by ignoring them but, more perniciously, by reading them as Stage 2. The fact that Stage 3 reasoners come to their decisions in structurally more complex ways than Stage 2 reasoners is ignored in the retrospective cynicism of social-scientific analysis. Rawls (1971) has pointed out that utilitarianism can always retrospectively read any principled moral decision as self-interest. As Radding (1979) argues in a similar context, such analyses dismiss the actors' plainly stated reasons for their actions.

Stage 3 institutions are characterized by the grouping of people, each of whom maintains mutual ties with the other members. Several excellent examples were created in medieval France, starting around the twelfth century: cities, towns, and communes; the aristocracy; the estates (*Staende*); and the "dualistic" system (*Staendestaat*) by which Rule was created through the cooperation of the *Staende* and the ruler. Each of these institutions was created from the same Stage 3 cooperation among elements. Pirenne (1952) explains how towns, for example, were integrated: "The burghers formed a corps, a *universitas*, a *communitas*, a *communio*, all the members of which, conjointly answerable to one another, constituted inseparable parts. . . . the city of the Middle Ages did not consist in a simple collection of individuals; it was itself an individual, but a collective individual, a legal person" (pp. 180–181). Poggi (1978, pp. 37–38) notes that this collective creation differed from earlier institutions based on dyadic ties of feudal vassalage. Each town formed a collective identity out of the individual equality of its citizens, and the old, Stage 2 relationship of feudal vassalage was banished in the towns: both Pirenne (1952, p. 193) and Poggi (1978, p. 40) note the German proverb *Stadtluft macht frei* (city air emancipates).

This joining together of equals is characteristic of other late medieval institutions. The landed aristocracy joined with the poorer knights in a solidarity of chivalry: "The consciousness of class which gradually caused the French aristocracy to become a homogeneous group was thus crystallized around the knightly ideal, its ethic and the virtues of wisdom and loyalty" (Duby, 1977, p. 180). This new association among the aristocracy was also made among towns. These associations were the estates (*Staende*)—again, a collective creation of formally equal and individually weak participants. The *Staende*, in turn, cooperated with the territory's ruler to create Rule. Rule was not exercised directly by the ruler as a right, but rather came from the cooperative association. This concept, often termed dualism, "suggests that the territorial ruler and the *Staende* make up the polity jointly, but as separate and mutually acknowledged political centers. Both constitute it, through their mutual agreement; but even during the agreement's duration they remain distinct, each exercising powers of its own, and differing in this from the 'organs' of the mature, 'unitary' modern state" (Poggi, 1978, p. 48).

The above passage leads us directly into the consideration of Stage 4 institutions, where the abstract principle of Rule is recognized as a prerequisite of social organization itself, not as a byproduct of mutual, bilateral agreement.[19] As Poggi (1978) puts it: "In the absolutist state the political process is no longer structured primarily by the continuous, legitimate tension and collaboration between two independent centers of Rule, the ruler and the *Staende*; it develops around and from the former only" (p. 68). Instead of being one of the centers of power whose "interpersonal" cooperation constituted a Stage 3 ideal relationship, the ruler is now the expression of Rule itself (see Poggi, 1978, chapter 4). The institutions built up from Stage 4 relationships are accordingly absolutistic in character: the modern army, bureaucracies (prior to Weberian rationality), absolute monarchies, fascist government, governments without civil liberties (i.e., subject to the domination of one group—"the tyranny of the majority"), and religions claiming absolute moral authority. Sacred custom, sacred law, sacred procedures, sacred religion—whatever the sacred system is, it constitutes a Stage 4 society. In Almond and Verba's (1963) terms, such societies are "subject" political cultures. Citizens are aware of and orient to the overarching moral authority represented by the state, but they have no sense that they themselves create and can alter that authority. Stage 4 conceptualizes society as a totality, and this permits great variability in institutional forms. As long as the institution establishes consistent role requirements, public support (ideally) will follow.

In France the transition to Stage 4 institutions can be seen in the reign of Louis XIV (1643–1715). Louis replaced the provincial feudal nobility with his own administrators and, by drawing the nobility to his court in Paris, made himself the arbiter of their fortunes. He thus replaced the Stage 3 feudal ties represented by the system of estates with Stage 4 direction from his single, overarching authority.[20]

Stage 5 relationships can be found in at least three institutions: constitutional democracy, as conceptualized by John Locke and Thomas Jefferson; capitalist market economy, as conceptualized by Adam Smith and his non-Marxian successors; and science, as conceptualized by Karl Popper. Note that these three institutions are ideal-typical; we make no claim that any particular society, including the United States, has institutions structured at this level.

Locke and Jefferson's theory of constitutional democracy presumes attitudes of mutual respect among citizens. Such respect makes possible the recognition of rights existing prior to a social contract—the "inalienable rights" of the Declaration of Independence. Such rights are inalienable because they are inherent in the preexisting moral relationship of mutual respect. The democratic (or representative) form of government reflects the relationship of mutual respect. In addition, the procedures for creating, administering, and adjudicating public law reflect the relationship of rational debate. The right of free speech and press and the right to petition Congress stem from the necessity of gathering all relevant information before a decision. Stage 5 rules of procedure are designed (or at least are evaluated in terms of our desire) to allow all sides to be heard. Due process in both execution and adjudication of laws reflects a desire to ensure that all interests have an opportunity to be heard.

The capitalist market economy, as seen by Adam Smith, also has these characteristics of mutual respect and rational debate. Mutual respect makes possible the basic agreements of the market system: the agreement upon everyone's right to buy and sell freely; the agreement upon an abstract medium of exchange; the agreement upon an impartial regulatory body of sufficient strength to preserve the conditions of free trade. What the relationship of rational debate was to constitutional democracy, the relationship of fair competition is to market economies. Fair competition allows all factors to be taken into account in a decision to buy or sell: the buyer or seller, like the rational debater, is provided with the entire range of alternatives from which to choose.[21]

Science resembles a free market system in that the "stock" (in the colloquial sense) of a theory rises or falls according to whether scientists "buy" it. Scientists start from a position of mutual respect, a recognition that their colleagues hold initially different beliefs and yet all seek scientific truth. This recognition enables scientists to work cooperatively toward their mutual goal, even though they may appear to be competing with one another on behalf of their own theories.[22] The procedures of scientific testing implement that co-operative spirit. Theories must be tested against real-world evidence through reproducible tests of hypotheses. The process is rational, in that hypotheses derived from "true" theories will be repeatedly confirmed and hypotheses of the other sort will at some time be disconfirmed. The criterion employed—that theory be able to predict empirical consequences—is acceptable to all concerned, and it is open enough to allow all relevant information to be gathered before a decision is made on a theory's validity.[23]

We will not speculate here about what institutions would reflect Stage 6 relationships. Kohlberg has not encountered such reasoning with sufficient frequency to prove empirically that it lies beyond Stage 5. Social institutions are invented when a group of people can relate to one another in the same way; accordingly, the development of Stage 6 institutions must await a larger concentration of Stage 6 reasoners. (Rawls, 1971, section 43, suggests possible governmental arrangements of the Just Society. The social forms discussed by Jackins, 1987, are also of interest in this connection.)

We are now in a position to test the present conceptualization against the three basic theoretical problems raised in the first part of this chapter: the locus of development, micro-macro connection, and normative grounding problems.

The Locus of Development and the Micro-Macro Connection

The locus of development problem is solved if "that which develops" in the conceptualization is at least ideally operationalizable. Is political culture, as we have defined it, at least ideally operationalizable? Clearly the cognitive structure of moral reasoning is operationalizable, as seen in Piaget's (1965), Kohlberg's (Colby and Kohlberg, 1987), and Rosenberg's (chapter 5) various methods. *Publicly common* reasoning structures can be measured by applying the same techniques to argumentation or action in a cultural context. This can be done most easily by studying cultural materials of public persuasion: pamphlets, speeches, public prayers, editorials, and so on. It can also be done, with some practical difficulty, by interviewing respondents in a cultural context, perhaps surrounded by their coworkers, children, boss, and mother-in-law. Because culture exists by virtue of publicly common understandings, researchers should be able to elicit it in coherent form.[24] The present conceptualization of political development accordingly solves the locus of development problem.

The problem of the micro-macro connection has been dealt with so extensively in this chapter that little more need be said. The micro-macro relationship is mediated by the cultural system, which interpenetrates, but is distinct from, both the individual system and the social system. Anticipated reactions link the individual and cultural systems, and institutions link the cultural and social systems. These relationships depend both on the cognitive level and on the conceptual content of the culture and its individual members. The cultural system does therefore connect the micro and macro levels of analysis, as Pye (1965, 1972) asserted.

Normative Grounding

Ways of relating are ethical systems, because ethics is the study of how people ought to relate to one another. Action within any specific way of relating implicitly ("always already," as Habermas puts it) raises a claim to the rightness of that action. Each different way of relating constitutes a different ethical system and is thus subject to ethical evaluation. A claim that people are to relate to one another in such and such a manner must be redeemed by normative argument. The normative issues raised by a theory of development must thus be considered.[25]

Even granted the existence of a universal developmental sequence of moral reasoning stages, the question can still be raised, is it *better* for a culture to be at a more advanced stage? This question is in fact two questions: first, is higher better for the moral reasoning of individuals; and second, is higher better for the political culture of a society? We take up these questions in turn.

First, is it morally better for an individual to employ a more developed stage of moral reasoning? After all, the empirical existence of a universal developmental sequence of moral reasoning does not prove each stage's ethical superiority over the prior stage. Even if the Piagetian psychological criteria of adequacy (comprehensiveness, differentiation, coordination: equilibration generally) show each stage more adequate than its predecessor, moral adequacy must be assessed on its own terms.

Kohlberg's sequence of stages represents (in Habermas's phrase) a "rational reconstruction" of moral development. The psychological theory and the normative theory on which it is grounded are linked, but distinct. The empirical results from the psychological theory (invariant sequence, stage consistency) can partially test, but cannot alone validate, the underlying normative theory, while the normative "an adequate psychological theory of stages and stage movement presupposes a normative theory of justice: first, to define the domain of justice reasoning and, second, to function as one necessary part of an explanation of stage development. For instance, the normative theoretical claim that a higher stage is philosophically a better stage is one necessary part of a psychological explanation of sequential stage movement" (Kohlberg, Levine, and Hewer, 1984c, p. 223).[26] Empirical falsification of the psychological theory would indicate that the normative theory (or the empirical method, of course) was flawed.

Kohlberg (1981a) defines moral adequacy in formalistic terms:

> I am arguing that a criterion of adequacy must take account of the fact that morality is a unique, *sui generis* realm. If it is unique, its uniqueness must be defined by general formal criteria, so my metaethical conception is *formalistic*. Like most deontological moral philosophers since Kant, I define morality in terms of the formal characteristics of a moral judgment, method, or point of view, rather than in terms of its content. Impersonality, ideality, universalizability, preemptiveness, and so on are the formal characteristics of a moral judgment. These are best seen in the reasons given for a moral judgment, a moral reason being one that has these properties. . . . [By using these

criteria] we can define a higher-stage judgment as "moral" independent of its content and of whether it agrees with our own
judgments or standards. (pp. 170–171)

This chapter's discussion of Kohlberg's stages uses these criteria
to argue the normative superiority of each stage to its predecessor.[27]
The stages are progressively more prescriptive (taking precedence
over a wider range of other, nonmoral concerns), more universal
(consistent when applied to a wider range of circumstances), and
more universalizable (consistent when binding on a wider range of
moral actors). The stages accordingly represent a hierarchy of moral
as well as psychological adequacy.[28]

The stages are easily misunderstood as evaluations of people (i.e.,
Stage 1 reasoners are bad, Stage 2 are a little better, Stage 6 are
saints). This is not a proper interpretation. In Kohlberg's (and our)
view, all people are acting morally, that is, in terms of their own
sense of morality. We cannot judge the actors as better or worse
people, but we can and do judge their moral reasoning as more or
less adequate, using the above standard criteria of moral reasoning.

The above discussion concerns the connection between "higher"
and "better" for individuals; the connection is made through use of
formal criteria. But clearly the same criteria are used for evaluating
the normative basis of political cultures. Both individual moral reasoning and political culture have as their subject the allocation of
rights and obligations among people in interaction with one another. The stages of individual moral reasoning show the varying
conceptions of how people ought to relate to one another mutually;
political culture shows which of these ways of relating can be carried out in practice.[29]

Political culture's connection to individual reasoning stages is not
surprising, because individual moral reasoning develops in interaction with the reasoning of others: problems with one's current stage
of reasoning appear as the problems of establishing and maintaining
cooperative relationships.[30] Political cultures develop in the same
manner: the problems (i.e., cognitive/moral conflicts) that, found in
social interaction, are the basis of individual moral development,
are also the basis of political cultural development. We shall see in

the next section of this chapter that the *dynamics* of political development are quite different from those of individual moral reasoning, because the conflicts are interpsychic rather than intrapsychic. Nevertheless, the *criteria* for the goodness of a political culture are the same as those for the goodness of an individual's moral reasoning. For this reason, and for the reasons cited earlier, we can fairly say that for a political culture to be more developed is in fact for it to be better.

The Dynamics of Development

The method just outlined—using a concept of public commonness to transform an individual-level theory of the development of moral reasoning into a macro-level conception of political development—also gives some sense of the dynamics of political development. Basically, development proceeds according to the interaction of two quite different forces: (1) the forces promoting or inhibiting wide-scale moral reasoning development; and (2) the forces promoting or inhibiting public commonness.

The former set of forces is fairly well understood: moral reasoning development is enhanced to the degree that people encounter, whether intellectually or practically, situations requiring a coordination of different moral perspectives. In a social setting, the necessity for such reasoning could arise through a variety of circumstances: exposure to higher-stage reasoning (during socialization or ordinary social interaction), or social conflicts which pit same-stage justifications against one another. The English civil wars, for example, confronted people on a wide scale with competing moral claims (and from our historical remove, virtually identical moral claims). When such conflicts are felt widely in the society, the potential for widespread moral development arises.

A pleasant implication of the present perspective is the absence of any natural force for political-developmental retrogression. Left to themselves, social actors would be expected to develop their moral reasoning to the degree necessary to resolve the moral claims among themselves.

There is another class of forces acting on developmental dynamics, however: those forces that govern whether a way of relating becomes (or remains) common, and then publicly common, in the society. Cultural interaction requires a choice among several alternative ways of relating, so the culture will depend both on what ways of relating are known and on their relative salience. The most obvious way of relating is whatever way of relating the culture has previously employed; thus, social inertia must be seen as the most significant force at work. Beyond inertia lies whatever forces regulate the salience of competing ways of relating. Here arise what we can call forces of hegemonic control: rewards and penalties differentially attached to alternative ways of relating, to increase or decrease their salience; control over channels of communications, particularly mass communications, to make alternative ways of relating better known or to keep them less well known; forces controlling socialization into this or that way of relating; and forces controlling those institutions responsible for cultural invention, such as think tanks, universities, corporations, and other subcultures, so that new ways of relating are invented only within certain limits.

What makes the process of social change and development appear so chaotic is that the forces of cognitive development are independent (both logically and, we believe, empirically) from the forces of inertia and hegemonic control. The multiplicity of moral conflicts already demands a quite complex theory for individual development and an even more complex one for aggregated individual development. This complexity is then further diffracted by the variety of hegemonic forces, which will be quite sensitive to institutional forms, technological stage, geography, history, and so on.

The virtue of the present perspective is that it gives analysts a "decoding device" for picking out specifically *developmental* changes from the general social flux. Without a focus for our studies, the field of social change becomes as chaotic as its subject. Big changes, small changes, changes in religion, family, party structure, political support, anomie, means of production, economic concentration, and so on ad infinitum: all have become grist for the mill of social change research, and the field stands in great danger of losing any overall meaning or coherence. But if our central concern is development, then the theoretical framework presented here puts these changes in perspective: we are most concerned with tracking the ups and downs of development, and other aspects of social change fall into place, receiving attention only to the degree that they affect development.

The Genetic-Epistemological Roots of Political Development

This chapter has ranged far afield from Piagetian psychology. This simply testifies to the power of Piaget's ideas, because the view of political development presented here owes its existence to the theoretical power of genetic epistemology.

The conceptualization of political culture employed here—the publicly common way of relating—solves by itself the locus of development and micro-macro connection problems. Since ways of relating are cognitive reasoning structures, as discussed earlier in the chapter, many theories of reasoning, Piaget's among them, would appear relevant. Thus, Piagetian genetic epistemology is sufficient to solve the first two theoretical problems of political development.

Several additional arguments lead us to believe that the Piagetian approach is also necessary for understanding political development. First, the micro-macro connection problem requires a recognition that people create their social institutions through publicly common ways of relating. As argued earlier, these ways of relating are constituted in social actors' publicly common reasoning systems, not simply publicly common rules or behavioral responses. Reasoning about how people are to relate to one another is ipso facto moral reasoning. For these reasons any theory of political development must contain a psychological theory of moral reasoning.

Second, the normative grounding problem requires normative evaluation of these reasoning systems. Other developmental theories (e.g., Vygotsky, 1978) currently do not provide the philosophical justification for such normative evaluations. It is true that some non-Piagetian theories of reasoning make normative judgments about the reasoning they observe: for example, Tversky's empirical work on choice contains a latent normative theory that people should choose rationally.[31] However, only Piagetian theories of reasoning are (a) developmental and (b) cross-culturally valid.

(a) Only genetic-epistemological theories explain the developmental origins of new reasoning systems. A normative theory of why one system is better than its predecessor is not a psychological theory of why people factually do create and adopt the better system. Thus, Tversky's theory of choice, for example, has no theory of why people invent, and choose to employ, more rational choice methods. Kohlberg's work contains such a theory as its explicit Piagetian heritage (Kohlberg, 1984) and has been tested longitudinally for over twenty years (Colby et al., 1983).

(b) Genetic-epistemological theories, of both normative and non-normative reasoning, have been extensively tested cross-culturally. (Cross-cultural tests of Kohlberg's work are cited in note 15, this chapter.)

We therefore conclude that only genetic-epistemological theories currently provide the psychological theory and cross-cultural validity (not to mention the normative support) required for a normative-psychological theory underlying a general political development conceptualization. No other theory of reasoning now exists that supports these claims.

_____

▬▬▬▬▬▬▬▬▬▬

Power and Political Consciousness

In the preceding three chapters we have pursued a sequence of studies which mark out three distinct research domains. Our focus began with a single political concept, for concepts are the most immediately identifiable elements out of which ideologies are built. Further research on individual concepts such as freedom, equality, community, legitimacy, power, rights, and so forth are necessary to fill out the array of concepts which are the common currency of political discourse. Although necessary, such a focus is only a preliminary step. Singular concepts clearly have intrinsic interest, and in certain contexts research may not need to move beyond a single concept, but such an approach is not sufficient if our goal is to provide a full understanding of the structure of political reasoning. Since political concepts are joined and, as development proceeds, interact, it is necessary to examine the ways in which concepts are interrelated. Thus, systemic analysis of the underlying structure of thought across a wide variety of content domains is essential. By the same token the analysis of individual concepts and an examination of the systemic qualities of thought must be accompanied by an analysis of the structural demands placed on individuals in particular political cultures and environments. Only when research advances along all three fronts will we begin to understand the behavioral consequences (if any) attendant upon differently structured belief systems.

It is our hope that our critical analysis of previous efforts and the new framework we have provided will convince other scholars to join us in developing all three research areas. Given the methodologies and the scope of our concerns, unless there is a major redirection of effort toward a Piagetian analysis of political thought, and unless our numbers begin to rival those following the Lockean paradigm, the wheels of political science will continue to spin in place upon faulty assumptions about the nature of human thought. It is also important that the concerns we raise not be limited to the field of belief systems. To the degree that political behavior is influenced by political thought, an inadequate understanding of the nature of belief systems will lead to an inadequate understanding of political behavior. Thus, as our knowledge of the structure of political thought deepens, other areas of concern to political scientists will be enriched. To illustrate, in this concluding chapter we offer our speculations on the ways in which belief structure, political consciousness, and power relations affect political behavior.

Power and Political Consciousness

The analysis of power over the past three decades has become increasingly sophisticated. Indeed, one could characterize progress in the field as the gradual elimination of disciplinary egocentrism. The early empirical studies of power followed an intuitive, symbolic approach based on attributions of power (Hunter, 1953). Citizens were simply asked to generate a list of people who were regarded as powerful, then the lists were compared in order to identify the powerful actors in the community. The reputational approach's conceptual flaws were easily identified. One individual might have a reputation for power which was unwarranted, while another individual might act beyond public view and thus not gain a reputation for power even though his or her power was substantial.

As the behavioral revolution gained influence, the discipline turned to the analysis of concrete acts of power (Dahl, 1961). The focus shifted to the immediately observable, surface elements in the exercise of power: actual decisions made by legitimate government officials. Who participated in decision making, and who benefited, became critical elements in the analysis. Ordinary citizens were of interest only to the extent that they became mobilized around particular issues. Since the political system was presumed to be open, nonparticipation did not loom large as an analytic problem. The "political" became that which produced conflict. If there were no observable conflicts, politics, and hence power, were not engaged.

Rather quickly, Bachrach and Baratz (1963) recognized that the exercise of power was not limited simply to decisions actually made. Perhaps even more relevant to the exercise of power were issues which were kept off the political agenda. Employing Schattschneider's concept of the mobilization of bias, Bachrach and Baratz argued that if individuals with vested interests in the status quo could prevent issues from arising which might challenge existing relationships, then their interests would not be put at risk in the decision-making process. That is, alongside participating in open political conflict, suppressing conflict should be considered a normal aspect of the exercise of power.

There are two aspects to power's "second face." First, according to the law of anticipated response, if a political actor is perceived as inordinately powerful, it is only rational not to expend political resources challenging existing relationships when there is little prospect of success. Thus, both issues and potential political actors are mobilized out of the political process. Second, passive preemption is not the only option available to the powerful. Active measures to coerce, co-opt, and manipulate are equally important. Thus, some issues will not be nurtured to the point of visible political conflict either because the powerful have employed resources to keep the issue off the political agenda, or because the relatively less powerful are not willing to risk limited resources in a conflict which has little hope of successful resolution, or because the costs of success are too high. From this perspective, nonparticipation becomes problematic, and the openness of the political system comes into question. Such considerations lead to the conclusion that in order to understand the exercise of power, the analysis must extend below the observable surface to examine the underlying mobilization of bias setting the political agenda (still the best study from this perspective is Crenson, 1971).

In sum, the analysis began with symbolic attributions, moved on to concrete observable actions, and then went a level below the surface to examine the forces determining which actions and interests became observable and articulated and which did not. Left unexamined was the manner in which power "influences, shapes or determines conceptions of necessities, possibilities, and strategies of challenge in situations of latent conflict" (Gaventa, 1980, p. 15). That is, the tools employed in the calculus of political action were assumed by the second-level analysts. The third level in the analysis of power, then, involves "locating the power processes behind the social construction of meaning . . ." (Gaventa, p. 15). Control of the means of political communication, and of the process of political socialization, forms a substantial part of the processes behind the social construction of meaning; but what distinguishes the third-level analysts' approach from previous attempts to understand power is the emphasis on the ways in which power alters political conceptions. Lukes (1974) and Gaventa (1980) underline the importance of *psychological adaptations* to power relations, and it is here that genetic epistemology can make a substantial contribution to further research.

It is commonplace to note that what you see depends on where you sit. The powerful and the powerless clearly have different perspectives, but there is more to the difference than a question of vantage point. The exercise of power has conceptual consequences for both the powerful and the powerless, but for the moment attention is drawn to the effects on those in subordinate roles. Many authors have noted that in a relationship marked by subjection and domination, those in subordinate positions have a tendency to internalize "the values, beliefs, or rules of the game of the powerful as a further adapative response" (Gaventa, 1980, p. 17). The colonized merge their persona with that of the colonizer, adopting beliefs, values, and even the dress of their European masters (Mannoni, 1956); the ideas of the ruling class are adopted by the ruled (Marx, 1848); prisoners in Hitler's concentration camps mimic their guards (Bettelheim, 1960); captives adopt the ideology of their captors (e.g.,

Patty Hearst); and the master's image of the slave becomes the slave's self-image (Katznelson, 1973).

With the exception of Marx's observation, these examples of internalization or identification tend to occur in "extreme situations" (Bettelheim, 1943) characterized by the subordinates' nearly complete helplessness to counteract the definitions of reality imposed by the powerful. In essence, the extreme situation creates a structure of infantilization which seeks to destroy individual identity, reducing the subordinate to childlike dependence on authority: "Being subject to such an external power reactivates very childish attitudes and feelings. Only in infancy did other persons, our parents, have the power to throw us into desperate inner turmoil if our wishes conflicted with theirs" (Bettelheim, 1960, p. 288). To escape that desperate inner turmoil, subordinates embrace the point of view of the powerful, making it their own, adjusting their behavior appropriately.

Extreme situations magnify the effect of power, but what is magnified is the tendency of all power to infantilize, to undermine self-direction and autonomy, producing compliant behavior and the acceptance of existing relations as legitimate (a classic example is Milgram, 1974). Thus, the focus on extreme situations is interesting not because those situations are unusual, but because they throw light on ordinary circumstances (Bettelheim, 1960, p. 108). In those ordinary circumstances, the powerful benefit whenever self-respect is eroded and replaced by the more primordial unilateral respect for authority characteristic of childhood structures of thought.

Like parents, the powerful have sanctions available to answer transgressions against the established order, and one readily available defense against those sanctions is to assimilate the moral codes of rulers into one's own belief system. In his masterful treatise on the social origins of obedience and revolt, Moore notes that there is "a widespread human tendency to interpret the clauses of the implicit social contract for the rulers' benefit" (Moore, 1978, p. 24). Even in cases where the rules of the game overwhelmingly favor elites, it is not the injustice of the rules which gives rise to rebellion, but the ruler's (or, for that matter, peers') failure to abide by the existing rules: "One of the most powerful sources of moral outrage is to see someone else getting away with breaking a moral rule one has undergone great pains to make a part of one's own character" (Moore, 1978, p. 36).

A most common form of adaptation in the face of inequalities of power, then, is the adoption of the powerful's definition of reality. Thus, the third-level analysts of power focus on the psychological adaptations of the powerless in the face of the powerful, and on how those adaptations tend to benefit the powerful. In the remainder of this chapter we identify the ways in which genetic epistemology might contribute to the analysis of those adaptations.

Genetic Epistemology Views
Power's Third Face

Our brief description of the third-level analysis has touched on several areas of central concern to genetic epistemology. When Gaventa writes of power's influence on "conceptions of necessities, possibilities, and strategies," he touches upon individuals' understanding of (1) relationships of cause and effect, (2) probability and prediction, (3) concepts of the future, past, and present, and (4) questions of what we might call sociopolitical transitivity; e.g., A is more powerful than B, B is more powerful than C, therefore A is more powerful than C; but B + C may (adding chance and probability to transitivity) be more powerful than A.

All four cognitive capacities have a direct bearing on action decisions. As individuals assess their situations, they will employ these various cognitive capacities in the construction of action schemas which they can mentally test before committing to action or inaction. The degree to which individuals reason from concrete to abstract, or from abstract to concrete, will influence the number of possible courses of action tested. If individuals view the existing reality as the only possible reality, few, if any, options will be assessed, and quiescence will likely result. On the other hand, the employment of abstract princples may lead to the conclusion that the existing reality comes up short in comparison to alternatives, and action designed to institute alternatives will be taken, provided the situation is deemed changeable. In short, as they survey the political terrain, individuals make political judgments about the pliability of power and the efficacy of individual or collective action, and they calculate the probable success of various action options.

The degree of cognitive complexity, relative role-taking skills, and moral judgments are also relevant considerations in trying to assess action judgments. For example, whether the powerless view the powerful as a unified whole or as riddled with divisions based on conflicting interests, and vice versa, is a consideration that taps the cognitive complexity dimension. If either group views the other as essentially without internal divisions, one set of tactics might be called for, while other tactics might be appropriate in the face of internal divisions on either side. Similarly, a divided opposition, in the face of a unified group of power-holders, might decide to abandon the field of battle. To some degree these calculations are affected by individuals' capacities to discriminate among members of a class. Hence, attention to those factors which inhibit or enhance cognitive complexity must be incorporated into the analysis. Environmental demands and experiences surely are among those factors (Lane, 1983), and different environmental demands and experiences may well have an impact on the rate and extent of the development of cognitive complexity.

For both the powerful and the powerless limited cognitive complexity surrounding power relations can serve an adaptive function. If the powerful view the powerless as an undifferentiated mass, stereotypes concerning the unsuitability of subordinates for the exercise of power can serve to rationalize the power inequality. From the other perspective, viewing the powerful as undifferentiated might serve an adaptive function in an environment in which the costs of challenging power are great. Even weak authorities would remain unchallenged because subordinates would view individual authorities through the template of the entire class of authorities, a class viewed as easily able to avert a challenge. Furthermore, the greater the environmental emphasis on hierarchy and the greater the sanctions for disobedience, the less likely an individual will be to develop the requisite autonomy to challenge authority, and the more likely the individual will be to view authorities as legitimate. Those at the bottom of the hierarchy are rewarded not for thinking, but for

obeying, and those on the lower rungs of the hierarchy are exposed
to only partial information. Thus, subordinates can rationalize inequalities of power with the comforting thought that those in authority have a better perspective from which to judge.

Not all power situations, of course, promote limited cognitive
complexity. Power-holders who face a sophisticated and well-orga-
nized opposition must be equally complex in their thinking if they
are to retain power. Otherwise, miscalculations or misperceptions
may lead to actions which actually undermine power. For the most
part, however, the reverse relationship is to be expected: subordinates with more egocentric perspectives facing authorities with
more differentiated and sociocentric perspectives. The reasons are
many, including the fact that the environments in which power-
holders generally operate make many more, and more varied, demands on cognitive capacities than do those in which the powerless
operate. But perhaps the most important reason is that subordinates
generally operate in environments which are far more anxiety-pro-
ducing. A modicum of anxiety can actually increase cognitive processing abilities, but beyond a certain minimal level, the effect of
anxiety is to close down mental processes (Rokeach, 1960). Intrinsic
to the exercise of power is the use or threat of sanctions, and therefore the exercise of power always produces anxiety among those
over whom it is exercised. When power is exercised over people
with little material security, the anxiety is likely to be great, and
when that exercise of power extends over long periods of time, the
effect is probably to constrain cognitive development. If Rokeach
(1960) is correct in arguing that closed belief systems are defenses
against anxiety, we should expect to find more egocentrism among
the powerless than among the powerful, as a direct function of the
anxiety produced by the exercise of power over them. (One exception to this expectation may be in situations in which two powerful
actors face each other, each with the capacity to destroy the other,
as in the case of the two superpowers. See White, 1984.)

When the powerless adopt the point of view of the powerful, then,
they are employing psychological adaptations which serve a defensive function. Here we raise an issue generally ignored in most approaches to the study of political belief systems: their purpose. Lane

(1986) has argued that there are two broad classes of purposes that political belief systems serve, which he labels consummatory and transactional. Transactional purposes lead the individual outside of the self to either change or understand the world. Consummatory purposes serve the self, providing pleasure. Each purpose is related to cognitive structure: "In an important sense, consummatory politics follows Piaget's egocentric pattern: Only what is in 'my' head is real and true. In another Piagetian sense, consummatory politics emphasizes assimilation, adjusting observations to prior schemata as contrasted to accommodation, adjusting schemata to fit observations. Transactional politics, on the other hand, implies an exchange with others, where reciprocity is important" (p. 304). The defensive functions of belief systems follow Lane's "cognitive pleasure principle": people assuage the pain from painful experiences either by distorting them to fit prior concepts in such a way that the painful aspects are suppressed, or by simply ignoring painful discrepancies completely. Consequently, consummatory politics are profoundly conservative, emphasizing stasis rather than the change served by transactional politics.

A particular community which over generations has experienced profound inequalities of power, and which has had severe sanctions imposed whenever transactional politics have been attempted, may well develop a political culture in which, in exchange for a meager degree of material security, inequalities of power are not only tolerated but legitimized and protected (e.g., Gaventa, 1980). When the meager security is not forthcoming, previous adaptations are thrown into disequilibrium, producing a reassessment of the terms of the implicit social contract. That is why, generally, it is after disruptions of the normal adaptations to everyday life—disruptions such as famine, strikes, war, or economic depressions—that rebellions occur (Moore, 1978).

Such calculations clearly involve anticipating responses to various actions both on the part of the powerful and on the part of the powerless, and this requires role-taking skills. The ability to place oneself in the position of another is a skill which develops over time and is related both to power relations and environmental constraints. As Piaget noted, role-taking is more difficult when there are extreme inequalities such as those between adults and children. Children therefore learn to role-play primarily in the context of peer relations. Situations marked by extreme inequalities of power may have the same effect on adults' ability to role-play. That is, if socialized in the context of subordination, particularly when that subordination includes little peer interaction, adults will exhibit little ability to role-play, with all attendant consequences, including unilateral respect for authority.

Environmental opportunities for role-playing are very much dependent upon power relations. In a society of equals, roles are fluid. In such a society, imagining oneself in the place of another requires only a small adjustment. With a more equitable distribution of positions of authority, ordinary people can reasonably expect that at some point over the course of their lives they will exercise authority, even though that authority may be limited. Similarly, in a complex society the choice of roles and the number of roles one can expect to play are much greater than in traditional societies with less complex divisions of labor. The greater the disparities of power and the fewer the available roles in a society, the fewer the incentives and the more difficult it becomes to step outside one's own particular position. Thus, the opportunities for role-taking presented by one's social location are, in critical ways, related to power distributions, and may well have a direct impact on the development of political cultures which either revere or challenge authorities.

Directly related to role-playing ability is the question of moral judgment. Either explicitly or implicitly, every political action involves a moral judgment. Both the action itself and the context in which the action takes place are subject to moral evaluations. Indeed, political actions are often the results of conclusions about the moral status of particular power relations. Choosing to boycott grapes in support of workers who are exposed to chemical pesticides, or to write a letter to government officials in protest of capital punishment, or to picket an abortion clinic, are obvious examples of morally charged political actions. The situation presents a moral issue, and the type of action chosen also involves a moral judgment. Rather than boycotting, writing, or picketing, individuals might also choose to destroy grape plants, assassinate political leaders, or blow up abortion clinics, and actions such as these are themselves subject to moral judgments. While these examples vividly highlight moral issues, even more mundane issues require attention to what is fair, what is right, what is moral. Moral issues are involved in such questions as, should voter registration be mandatory or voluntary, should homeowners be allowed to remodel their homes as they please, and should children be required to learn how to swim as a condition of graduation; and how one goes about pressuring authorities to adopt a particular solution involves a moral judgment about appropriate action. Thus, both the way in which one judges a power relationship, and the action or inaction one chooses in response, clearly involve moral reasoning.

The question from the point of view of genetic epistemology is: how do differences in the quality of moral judgments affect the way in which one conceives political dilemmas and the types of solutions one pursues? The considerable research on the impact of moral reasoning on political behavior has produced mixed results. In a study of Berkeley political activists Haan, Smith, and Block (1968) found that those who scored highest on Kohlberg's scale were the most politically active and were particularly active in dissident politics, challenging those in power. Interestingly, males who scored low on Kohlberg's scale also tended to be active in radical politics. Those who scored in the middle of the scale were described as having harmonious, nonskeptical relations with traditional institutions and with authorities. These individuals were also conservative both in their personal lives and in politics. Kohlberg (1968) has found that levels of moral reasoning predicted who would refuse to obey authority in the context of Milgram's learning experiment. But other studies have been less successful in predicting, for example, who would cheat on an exam (Kohlberg and Candee, 1983). These conflicting results may be a function of situational effects as well as differences in behavioral consequences. But the studies do seem to point to the conclusion that high levels of moral reasoning are required to challenge authority (with the exception noted above). Unless one regards authority as fallible, unless one has command of a language of defiance, unless one has self-esteem, and unless one acts on the basis of principled autonomy, power remains unmolested.

People in positions of subordination marked by extreme inequalities of power are not likely to possess those qualities.

Command hierarchies do not value independent thinking. By definition, command hierarchies do not value individual autonomy. Only in the most extreme circumstances are subordinates in command hierarchies expected to regard authorities as fallible. Although less rigid than command hierarchies, the reward structure and the customary ways of relating in most hierarchies reinforce deferential attitudes toward authority. Similarly, in an environment in which "superior" people occupy positions of authority, and "inferior" people occupy subordinate positions, it is difficult for the latter to develop a sense of self-esteem which can sustain an individual through the process of challenging authority. Thus, all of the environmental messages lead to the conclusion that the existing order is a just order, and morality is defined in terms of subscribing to established ways of relating. Even if outside observers might regard the established structure as fundamentally immoral, those within the system have adjusted their observations to fit prior schemata, schemata formed under pressure from power configurations.

The central question is whether or not particular power relations in a particular environment are such that the cognitive structure of individuals in subordinate positions is altered or retarded *as a result* of the exercise of power. There are numerous examples of the content of belief systems changing as one's position in a power hierarchy changes. For example, in one study workers were interviewed about their attitudes toward authority on the job and about the appropriate role of workers in decision making. The same workers were reinterviewed after they were promoted to management positions. As might be expected, their views shifted considerably in favor of management prerogatives once they were in positions of authority. Economic cycles intervened and a reorganization of the workplace resulted in the demotion of the recently promoted employees. When interviewed a third time, their views had reverted to a position antagonistic to management. Thus, it is clear that the content of beliefs can be affected by changes in one's position in a status hierarchy. Left unanswered is the question of whether or not cognitive structures were similarly affected.

Lukes and Gaventa in their emphasis on psychological adaptations to power relations assert that power actually changes concepts, but for the most part their concern is with the changes in the conceptual content, not changes in conceptual structure. Genetic epistemology can help explain how the conceptual changes occur, whether or not such change is a function of cognitive structure, and whether or not it is the cognitive structure which changes. Several examples we might include under the rubric of identification with the aggressor were cited in the preceding pages, pointing to the ways in which subordinates internalize authority's perspective. The question to which we turn now is whether or not this internalization is a function of cognitive structure.

From the Piagetian perspective there are at least two theoretical possibilities which might lead to an explanation of the processes by which subordinates adopt the point of view of those who exercise authority over them. Abstract logic necessary for taking up a critical stand toward existing relations is available only to individuals who have passed through a series of developmental stages, in which the necessary cognitive operations are slowly and laboriously constructed and fashioned into an interrelated system of thought. Throughout that process of development the self gradually becomes distinct from the environment. Environments which undermine individuation, limit self-esteem, restrict autonomy, and break down the bonds among peers while reinforcing attachments to authorities may retard the developmental process, leaving individuals without the necessary intellectual skills or inclination to challenge authority. Under such conditions the self is embedded in a particular set of social relations which define it. Alterations in those social relations consequently produce alterations in self-definitions. Consistent self-substantiation, then, is dependent upon consistent authorities and social relations. The continuous self thus becomes a function of the existing power relations, and an attack on that order becomes an attack on the self. In sum, one major hypothesis to be tested is whether or not the tendency of adult subordinates to embrace the view of authorities is a function of socialization in hierarchies that retard intellectual development by promoting dependence, other-directedness, and de-differentiation.

A second theoretical possibility is that the adoption of the point of view of authorities is a function of a cognitive regression. Presented with a new situation which produces high levels of anxiety or threat, an individual who had already advanced to higher levels of cognitive functioning might respond by functioning at a much lower cognitive capacity. This should be a relatively rare occurrence, and developmental retardation should be more frequent than regression, but there is some evidence that cognitive regressions take place. The clearest evidence is associated with aging and with mental illness. Feffer (1967) and Looft (1971, 1972), have shown how egocentrism can be a symptom expression in mental illness, and that over the life span, very elderly individuals living in relative isolation tend to lose cognitive skills beginning with the most lately developed ones. Under these conditions, cognitive development "unwinds," but researchers have not yet paid sustained attention to whether or not otherwise healthy adults might be similarly affected by either traumatic events or extended subordination in a power hierarchy. The closest "laboratories" for the examination of this possibility are the techniques of "brainwashing" in which affect is manipulated, generally under conditions of social isolation, to undermine the established belief system and replace it with beliefs preferred by the brainwashers. It may be that some social structures act upon individuals in similar ways. Genetic epistemology, then, presents the analysis of power with a whole new set of questions and new ways of approaching adaptations to power. While the methodological demands are greater and the time commitment longer than for studies based on mass surveys, the rewards are potentially much greater.

Appendix: Piaget's Use of Egocentrism

1   "Infantile egocentrism is thus in its essence an undifferentiation between self and social environment."
2   "Egocentrism is by definition the confusion between self and the other."
3   "It is somehow the totality of precritical and consequently pre-objective attitudes of knowledge."
4   "Egocentrism consists only in taking as sole reality the one which appears to perception."
5   "It is the negation of the objective attitude, consequently of logical analysis. It leads on the contrary to subjective synthesis."
6   "Egocentrism ought not to be defined only by the primacy of assimilation over accommodation, but by its disequilibrium of the two processes, with primacy alternating between one and the other."
7   "The thought of the young child was egocentric, not in the sense of a hypertrophy of the self, but in the sense of centration on his own point of view."
8   "We call egocentrism the undifferentiation of one's own point of view and that of others."
9   "Childish egocentrism, far from being asocial, always goes hand in hand with adult constraint. It is presocial only in relation to cooperation."
10 "Egocentrism appears to us as an intermediate between socialized and purely individual behavior."
11 "[The child] plays in an individual manner with material that is social; such is egocentrism."
12 "Egocentrism is opposed to objectivity, as far as objectivity means relativity on the physical plane and reciprocity on the social plane."

Most of these definitional statements are taken from *Piaget: Dictionary of Terms*, by Antonio M. Battro.

13   "Egocentrism is an effect characterized by an undifferentiation between the subject and his exterior world, and not by the exact knowledge which the subject has of himself: instead of leading to an effort of introspection or reflection, upon the self, infantile egocentrism is on the contrary ignorance of the interior life and deformation of the self as well as ignorance of objective relations and deformations of things."

14   "Social egocentrism is an epistemic attitude as well as purely intellectual egocentrism; it is a way of understanding others, as egocentrism in general is an attitude toward objects."

15   "One quality stands out in the thinking of the young child: he constantly makes assertions without trying to support them with facts. This lack of attempts at proof stems from the character of the child's social behavior at this age, i.e., from his egocentricity conceived as a lack of differentiation between his own point of view and that of others. It is only vis-à-vis others that we are led to seek evidence for our statements."

16   "Certain features of child morality always appear to be closely connected with a situation that from the first predominates in childhood (egocentrism resulting from the inequality between child and adult surroundings which presses upon him) but which may recur in adult life, especially in the strictly conformist and gerontocratic societies designated as primitive."

17   "Egocentrism and imitation are one and the same."

18   "However dependent he may be on surrounding intellectual influences, the young child assimilates them in his own way. He reduces them to his point of view and therefore distorts them without realizing it, simply because he cannot yet distinguish his point of view from that of others through failure to co-ordinate or 'group' the points of view. Thus, both on the social and on the physical plane, he is egocentric through ignorance of his own subjectivity."

19   "Intellectual egocentricity is nothing more than a lack of co-ordination, a failure to 'group' relations with other individuals as well as with other objects."

20   "The initial absence of substantive objects is the first example of the transition from primitive, total egocentricity to the final elaboration of an external universe."

21   "In accordance with a law we have already seen manifested in the infant and the young child, each new mental ability starts off by incorporating the world in a process of egocentric assimilation. Only later does it attain equilibrium through a compensating accommodation to reality. The intellectual egocentricity of adolescence is comparable to the egocentricity of the infant who assimilates the universe into his own corporal activity and to that of the young child who assimilates things into his own nascent thought (symbolic play, etc.). Adolescent egocentricity is manifested by belief in the omnipotence of reflection, as though the world should submit itself to idealistic schemes rather than to systems of reality. It is the metaphysical age *par excellence*; the self is strong enough to reconstruct the universe and big enough to incorporate it."

22 "We have seen how these successive constructions always involve a decentering of the initial egocentric point of view in order to place it in an ever-broader coordination of relations and concepts, so that each new terminal grouping further integrates the subject's activity by adapting it to an ever widening reality."

23 "Far from helping the subject distinguish between his own and other viewpoints, the egocentric attitude tends to encourage him to accept it without question as the only one possible."

24 "Each for himself, and all in communion with the 'Elder': such might be the formula of egocentric play."

25 "When assimilation outweighs accommodation (i.e., when the characteristics of the object are not taken into account except insofar as they are consistent with the subject's momentary interests) thought evolves in an egocentric or even autistic direction."

Notes

Chapter 1

1 While there are important similarities between Piaget's structuralism and the continental structuralism which grew out of Saussure's work on language, there are three important points of divergence. First, structuralism focused on the static qualities of thought, its basic binary oppositions. As suggested by his first assumption, Piaget focused on thought as an activity. In this context he might view the oppositions addressed by structuralism as a subjectively constructed product. Second, structuralism was idealist. Thought was viewed simply as a quality of mind. Piaget's pragmatism attempted to bridge the gap between idealism and realism. Thus, for Piaget, thought was embedded in reality. This second difference underlies the third. The structuralists see thought as static, as a reflection of mind. Piaget sees the structure of thought in relation to reality and hence as a developmental phenomenon.

2 For a more detailed discussion of the epistemological bases of Piaget's theory of cognitive development, see chapter three of Rosenberg's *Reason, Ideology and Politics* (1988b).

3 For examples of Piaget's consideration of the impact of social environments, see Piaget (1965, 1966).

4 For another discussion of the impact of social environments on cognitive development, see Rosenberg (1988b, chapter 4).

5 For a classic definition of attitudes, see Allport (1935).

6 For reviews of the literature, see Wicker (1969). A response to the problem in the social-psychological research was to suggest that attitudes were too broadly conceived and the complexity of the context in which behaviors were performed were not appreciated in the early research. In this vein Fishbein and others have suggested formulations in which attitudes toward specific behaviors under par-

ticular conditions are assessed. This research does generate better attitude-be-havior correlations but at great cost to the generality of the descriptive concepts they used. For example, see Fishbein (1974).

Chapter 2

1   The argument on pp. 22–30 was first presented as part of a paper by Shawn Rosenberg, "The Structural Developmental Analysis of Political Thinking: An Alternative to the Belief Systems Approach," delivered at the 1982 annual meeting of the American Political Science Association, Denver. The argument is developed further in chapter 2 of Rosenberg (1988b). The remainder of the argument was first presented in a paper by Dana Ward, "Genetic Epistemology and the Structure of Belief Systems: An Introduction to Piaget for Political Scientists," also delivered at the 1982 annual meeting of the American Political Science Association.

2   It is noteworthy that in adopting this approach Converse and those following in his footsteps have rejected a more sociological alternative in which political understanding and evaluation is studied with reference to the collective rather than the individual (e.g., Lukacs, 1968; Geertz, 1964; Althusser, 1971).

3   Here again it is unfortunate that Converse's characterizations are so sketchy. In explicating the nature of social constraint he does suggest that the mass public learns how to think about politics through exposure to the ideological conceptions made available to them by political elites. He does not, however, characterize the nature of this learning process nor does he comment on the origin of the elite's ideological conceptions.

4   While to some Converse's "oversight" in imposing the liberal/conservative dimension may appear an inexplicable error in the midst of otherwise well-conceived research, the decision is quite compatible with his view of belief systems as socially constrained. Assuming that the liberal/conservative dimension structures the elite belief system (there is, however, no evidence to suggest it does, and some of Converse's evidence suggests it does not), then whatever integration the belief systems of mass publics evidence should be organized around that dimension. Consequently, factor analysis and its often uninterpretable results may be justifiably avoided.

5   It should be noted that open-ended questions do offer the subject some opportunity to justify or explain expressed opinions and thus to clarify the meaning of the connections he or she makes. Our complaint is that subjects do not offer enough comment of this kind spontaneously, nor does the researcher probe sufficiently to extract the required information. Nonetheless, insofar as some justifications are offered, the data may be more confidently interpreted than the inter-item correlations. What comparative advantage may be gained by relying on the open-ended question format is lost in research that interprets the data through the use of computer searches of key words (Field and Anderson, 1969;

Nie et al., 1976). In this case the subject's response is coded on the basis of specific references made and without regard to the nature of the connections he or she forges among the entities mentioned.

6   The criticism developed here should demonstrate the futility of Nie, Verba, and Petrocik's defense of their continued use of constraint on the grounds that they know of no alternative ideologies that would explain contradictory responses (1976; 1979, p. 27). The problem with their approach is the complete lack of *any* psychological theory. This is particularly surprising in light of their claim that psychological forces are a central part of their endeavor (pp. 6–7). Their approach is strictly political.

Chapter 3

1   For further discussion of the Lockean epistemological foundations of the belief systems research and the contrasting foundations of the Piagetian research, see Rosenberg, 1983; 1988b, chapters two and three.

2   An example might help to explain how assimilation and accommodation always occur together, and I shall use the example given by Flavell. (As is true of all the concepts introduced, Flavell treated them in much greater detail, and no reader can fail to profit from his exposition.) In order for us to eat and thereby maintain ourselves we must accommodate ourselves to the form in which the nourishment we require is found in the environment. At the simplest level there must be some entry to our organism: the mouth. When we open our mouths to allow food to pass we are making an accommodation, just as we do when we move our jaws to chew the food. But simultaneously we are assimilating the food, preparing it for digestion as it passes through the mouth and as we chew. In addition, our digestion process must accommodate the food's specific chemical and physical properties in order to assimilate it. Thus, through the assimilative process of nourishing ourselves we must simultaneously accommodate ourselves to the nourishment: "The organism must accommodate its functioning to the specific contours of the object it is trying to assimilate" (Flavell, 1963, p. 45).

3   This is a point Vygotsky also makes: "Development, as often happens, proceeds here not in a circle but in a spiral, passing through the same point each new revolution while advancing to a higher level" (Vygotsky, 1978, p. 56).

4   There is some question as to exactly how one should divide the system, since concrete operational and formal operational thought are both forms of operational thought and therefore sometimes are seen as forming subperiods of a single period. Even though the difference between sensorimotor and preoperational thought is greater than that between concrete and formal thought, it still makes sense to think in terms of the fourfold division portrayed here. On this issue we are deviating from Flavell, who treats concrete and formal operations as subperiods of a single operatory period rather than as periods proper. Piaget

(1962) distinguished intelligence in terms of "four great periods in the development of intelligence," and it is this cue which is followed here.

5 Ages are all relative; the point is the order of succession, not the precise age at which the child develops the various structures. If ages were absolute, we would be dealing with maturation, not the construction of intelligence, and environment could be ignored.

6 Freud's "Project for a Scientific Psychology," which is also referred to as "Psychology for Neurologists," in which Freud hoped to discover the neurological basis of psychological phenomena, can be found in the *Standard Edition of the Complete Psychological Works of Sigmund Freud.* The 1844 manuscripts can be found in the collected works of Marx and Engels.

7 Perhaps this is an appropriate place to say egocentrism does not mean narcissism, and the reader is advised not to think of egocentrism in the terms in which it is often used in common parlance. Specifically because of this confusion between the "scientific" and "popular" uses of terms, Piaget, referring to the development of representational thought and the symbolism centering on the self, commented: "We no longer call it 'egocentric,' as one of us once did, in deference to the criticisms from many psychologists who are still not familiar with the practice in the exact sciences of using a term only in accordance with the definitions proposed, irrespective of its popular meanings and associations" (Piaget and Inhelder, 1969, p. 61). After absorbing this slap on the hands, perhaps we might prepare ourselves to employ the scientific practice. Thus, in deference to Piaget we continue to use egocentrism as he developed the term; but not without some sense of conflict. Generally, it is a good policy to use terms easily communicable to the uninitiated if we are to communicate our findings to the nonspecialist public. But since we have a perfectly adequate substitute in common use—narcissism—perhaps we might exercise a leadership function by presenting a distinction between narcissism and egocentrism: the one an affective term, the other a cognitive one.

8 For a definition of stage that applies well to Piaget's concept, see Habermas (1979, pp. 73–75). The reader is cautioned, however, that in the second characteristic Habermas (or his translator) refers to stages as "irreversible." Surely it should read "invariant," since there can be structural deterioration; e.g., see Feffer (1967) and Looft (1972). For other treatments of stages, see Kohlberg (1969) or Inhelder (1953).

9 There is a tendency among some interpreters of Piaget (e.g., Flavell) to treat development in a teleological manner; that is, there is a predefined goal toward which development proceeds. That is not the interpretation here and it is not how the word "goal" is employed. The "goals" are simply the empirically identifiable equilibrium points of a particular stage of development. In this view, evolution is an open-ended process, even if the functions of adaptation and organization remain invariant. Thus, for example, in the area of moral reasoning there need not be simply three stages (as in Piaget's system) or six (as in Kohl-

berg's refined system). As others have suggested (e.g., Habermas and Fishkin), there now seems to be developing a seventh stage. The reason there can be no end state is that "progress"—that is, change—is ensured by the dialectic between assimilation and accommodation. While stages, systems, and structures have a certain strength, the seeds of transformation—inadequacies, lattice vacancies (see C. S. Smith, in Weschler, 1978), and so forth—are contained within each structure, propelling the organism, or the organization of intellect, to ever finer resolutions of, or adaptation to, reality. Reality itself is infinitely expandable and is itself changed by our activity. Much of this can be accounted for in Gödel's proof. At any rate, there is no static, fixed goal to development in any teleological sense.

10 For more on role-taking, see Feffer (1959); Feffer and Gourevitch (1960); Feffer and Suchotliff (1966); Cowan (1966); Flavell (1966); Flavell, Botkin, Fry, and Wright (1968); Kohlberg (1971); and Rottenberg (1974).

11 Since dogmatism as measured by the D scale (Rokeach, 1960) is synchronic, and egocentrism is diachronic, the exact correspondence will be difficult to establish. But there should be a correlation, for example, between stage four—law and order orientations on Kohlberg's scale of moral reasoning—and dogmatism.

12 The best compilation of research on Piaget's theory is Modgil (1974).

13 Both of these quotations point to possible operationalized measures of the structures of beliefs and to important areas that would need to be included in studying correlates of adult egocentrism. For example, social isolation ought to correlate with egocentrism if it is indeed the case that evidence is sought only vis-à-vis others. In addition, the failure to entertain alternative viewpoints, or the tendencies to assert rather than to argue and give evidence, ought to prove crucial categories of analysis.

14 One example is the research on student activists during the 1960s and 1970s. See Fishkin, Keniston, and McKinnon (1973); Haan (1968); Kohlberg (1964); and Patterson (1975). It also might be added that Gilligan's work (1982) shows clear political relevance. Her critique of Piaget and Kohlberg (1982) has substantial merit, and must be incorporated, but her work remains within the same paradigm as theirs.

Chapter 4

1 Only the two oldest children were interviewed for a number of reasons. There were limited funds, and interviewing all of the children would have doubled costs and the time involved. More important, there were considerable differences in family size. Roughly half of the men had only two children, while the other half averaged six children. Thus, any group comparisons would be skewed by the different family sizes. In addition, several of the children were quite young, still in the formative stages of their belief systems, and this too would have made comparisons difficult. Finally, I wanted to compare the second gener-

ation to the first generation from roughly similar points in each generation's life cycle. As it was, the first generation had been approximately eight years older when Lane interviewed them than the second generation when I interviewed them.

2 As originally conceived, the interviews with the children constituted part of a three-pronged project. Other investigators were to reinterview the original men and interview the men's wives for the first time. At this time the fathers have been reinterviewed, but the interviews with the wives have not been conducted. The full study of the children can be found in Ward (1981).

3 From the Greek *demos* meaning "the people" and *archia* meaning "rule." Rejai (1967, p.2) tells us that the word was coined by Herodotus in the fifth century B.C.

4 For relevant research in this area, see Adelson and O'Neil (1966); Adelson (1971); Adelson, Green, and O'Neil (1969); Gallatin and Adelson (1970); Adelson and Beall (1970); Berg and Mussen (1975); Cowan, Langer, Heavenrich, and Nathanson (1969); Easton and Dennis (1965); Easton and Hess (1962); Hess (1963); Jahoda (1959, 1963, 1964); Kohlberg (1963a, 1963b, 1964, 1969); Neugarten (1949); Piaget and Weil (1951); Siegal (1970); and Zellerman and Sears (1971).

Chapter 5

1 This chapter reports the first of series of studies conducted by Rosenberg on political reasoning. The present study was conducted in the summer of 1980 and was first reported at the 1981 annual meeting of the International Society of Political Psychology and later at the 1982 Annual Meeting of the American Political Science Association. For a report of later research which continues the inquiry on the relationship between political and nonpolitical thinking, see Rosenberg, 1987. For additional structural developmental research on other aspects of political thinking, see Rosenberg (1988a).

2 For a full elaboration of the view of Piaget presented here, see Rosenberg (1988b, chapter three).

3 Early evidence on the failure of adults to reach formal operational thought was provided in research on thinking among members of tribal or peasant cultures. For example, see Peluffo (1967); Prince (1968); Luria (1976); and Dasen (1977). More recently, similar results have been achieved in the study of American adults. See Sinnott (1975); Kuhn et al. (1977); Long et al. (1979).

Piaget's short response (1972) to the criticism engendered by this research, that perhaps not everyone reached formal operational thought in all domains of thinking, was plainly inadequate. He failed to consider the implications of the claim that a structure might never generalize for his general theory. In addition, he simply ignored the evidence on failure to achieve concrete operational thinking.

4 See Piaget (1965b, 1971).

5   For a more complete and recent definition of the three stages, see Rosenberg (1988b, pp. 102–58).

Chapter 6

1   Hobhouse (1906); Habermas (1979b); Kohlberg (1981a); Radding (1979, 1985); Doebert (1981); and, according to some readings, Hegel (1975).

2   In particular, the theorist must point to a highest, or ideal, state of development in order to eliminate development theories that merely tinker with a basic injustice. Such theories may form part of a more comprehensive, fully grounded theory, of course.

3   This trichotomy is taken from Lehman's (1972) work, which in turn is based on Parsons (e.g., 1961). Parsons calls the individual system the "personality system." The three Parsonian systems are paralleled by or reproduced in the speech functions listed in Habermas's "Universal Pragmatics." Parsons's individual system is the locus of what Habermas refers to as " 'my' world of internal nature" (1979a, p. 68), where the sole validity claim is that one is truthful in expressing one's own subjective nature; Parsons's cultural system is the locus of what Habermas refers to as " 'our' world of society," where the sole validity claim is that one communicates rightly in the context of a legitimate interpersonal relationship; and Parsons's social system is the locus of what Habermas refers to as " 'the' world of external nature," where the sole validity claim is that one communicates the truth in attempting to represent facts.

4   Almond's (1956) original definition of political culture can be read as referring to the cultural system, but it was modified in Almond and Verba (1963) to fit the latter study's survey methodology.

5   Chilton (1988a), employing a battery of nine theoretical criteria for the concept of political culture, demonstrates that this definition is admissible and that previous definitions of political culture are not.

6   Unfortunately, such research sometimes studies individual characteristics instead of relationships.

7   Elias (1978) carefully describes the changes in the courtesy system. Elias (1982) discusses the association of these cultural changes with political structure changes.

8   One major reason why experiments with Prisoner's Dilemma-type games are difficult to control is that the culture of the experimental context is poorly defined and can be altered ("cued") quite by accident.

9   The third group was an outcast group, disliked and disesteemed by both others.

10   This does not mean people stopped being racist. What it does mean is that people had to worry about publicly expressed condemnation (the cultural system) and federal law enforcement (the social system) when committing criminal racist acts.

11   There may have been a slow change in individuals over a period of a century, but

slow change cannot account for the rapid evolution of the movement in the early 1960s.

12   Habermas (1983) discusses how the theoretical status of social science is affected by the unique necessity of social scientists studying action schemas in what he calls the "performative attitude." He also discusses the role that justification in discourse plays in social action.

13   Flavell (1968), Selman (1971), Piaget (1977), Habermas (1979, especially pp. 6–129), Higgins, Ruble, and Hartup (1983), and Overton (1983) discuss various aspects of the general connection among moral reasoning, role-taking, and social behavior. Berti, Bombi, and Lis (1982) and Berti, Bombi, and De Beni (1986) describe the Piagetian developmental acquisition of economic conceptions about means of production, owners, and profit. Habermas (1975, 1979) has been particularly concerned with the connection among social behavior, moral reasoning, and the state's ability to legitimize its rule. See Piaget (1965), Kohlberg (1984a), and Colby et al. (1983) for general discussions of the moral development research tradition. See Kohlberg (1981) and Kohlberg, Levine, and Hewer (1984c) for a discussion of the claims presented here. Attacks on these claims can be found in Fishkin (1982), Gilligan (1982), Gibbs (1977), and other authors cited in Kohlberg, Levine, and Hewer (1984b). The latter work contains Kohlberg's replies.

All that this present work requires is that some sequence of stages satisfy the five claims given in the text. (This statement implies neither agreement nor lack of agreement with Kohlberg's critics. Ward, Rosenberg, and Chilton differ somewhat among themselves in their assessment of the specifics of Kohlberg's work.)

14   The stages of moral reasoning are most emphatically not evaluations of people's moral worth. A person employing Stage 1 reasoning is no less and no more worthy of respect for his or her claims to moral treatment than a person employing the fabled Stage 6 reasoning. Just as philosophers critique one another's positions as being ambiguous and having unfortunate implications, without thereby condemning one another as evil people, so does the sequence of stages systematize and abstract the critiques of reasoning structures without thereby condemning the various researchers (Kohlberg, 1981, especially parts 1 and 2).

15   Readers not already familiar with Kohlberg's work should see Chilton (1988b), Kohlberg (1981c, 1984b), and especially Colby and Kohlberg (1987) for the exact stage definitions.

16   Note once again that the discussions below neglect non-Western institutions. As mentioned earlier, the limitation here arises from the principal author's ignorance of non-Western societies, not from the basic theory of moral reasoning development.

17   Note that punishment of miscreants' families occurs in many early legal systems. See Bloch (1961) on the medieval European vendetta, and Hobhouse (1906, chapter three) for examples from many other cultures.

18   See Bloch (1961) and Poggi (1978) for a discussion of the specifics of feudal relationships. Hear Poggi's (1978) description of the hierarchical extension of

Stage 2 feudal relations: "Historically, however, the elaboration of the lord-vassal relationship mostly advanced *downward*. Typically, a territorial ruler, finding it impossible to operate a system of rule constituted of impersonal, official roles, sought to bridge the gap between himself and the ultimate objects of rule—the populace—by relying primarily on his retinue of trusted warriors. To this end, he endowed them with fiefs from the landed domain under his charge . . . but his immediate vassals often carved from their own fiefs smaller ones for the members of their retinues" (pp. 24–25).

19   Wolin (1960) makes this point in his discussion of Hobbes.

20   See Deutsch, Dominguez, and Heclo (1981, pp. 189–91). Thomas Wright (1984) presents a study of the first Ibañez administration in Chile that shows striking parallels between Ibañez's and Louis XIV's methods.

21   A distinction must be made here between capitalism as a philosophical system, which requires Stage 5 structure, and capitalism as mere marketplace behavior, which requires only Stage 2 structure. The latter is more apparent to us, since most of our economic behavior involves mere evaluations of immediate self-interest as we buy or sell (Lane, 1983). But capitalism as a philosophical system also requires a common commitment of all producers and consumers to preserving the systemic characteristics (many producers, many consumers, free prices, sanctity of contract, etc.) that are required for capitalism to provide the happy results attributed to it (national wealth, market clearing, maximally efficient use of resources, people rewarded according to their deserts, liberty, etc.). Such a common commitment is justified by, and thus arises out of, a Stage 5 understanding of the connection between alternative marketplace rules and social benefits.

22   Just as Adam Smith saw entrepreneurs cooperatively benefiting society, even though they appeared to compete for good and profits.

23   Thomas Kuhn (1970a, 1970b) called this form of science "Normal Science."

24   See Chilton (1988a) for further discussion of how cultural ways of relating might be measured. We say that researchers "should be able" to elicit cultural materials, but the phrase obviously hides a lot of hard work. The long training and difficult fieldwork of cultural anthropologists illustrate the practical and mental difficulties involved. The present question, however, is whether such study is possible at all, not whether it is easy.

25   For a discussion of the necessary connection between ways of relating and ethical questions, see Habermas (1979a, 1979b) and McCarthy (1979). For a careful refutation of cultural relativists' and moral relativists' attempts to disconnect ways of relating from ethical questions, see Kohlberg (1981).

26   See also Habermas (1983).

27   See also the discussion in Kohlberg (1984b) and Kohlberg (1981a, 1981b).

28   As might be guessed, the claim of increasing moral adequacy is disputed in various ways. Gibbs (1977), for example, claims that Stage 6 reasoning may differ from, but is not better than, Stage 5 reasoning. Gilligan (1982) claims that

Kohlberg's scoring system ignores forms of moral reasoning often employed by women. There are at least three successive lines of defense against such attacks. The first is simply a "hard-boiled Kohlbergian" claim that such attacks are mistaken. Space does not permit the joining of such a dispute here; the reader should consult Kohlberg, Levine, and Hewer (1984c).

The second line of defense is a more flexible, genetic-epistemological claim that even if Kohlberg's specific sequence is incorrect (say, because it misreads women's reasoning), this will be revealed by anomalies in longitudinal studies and subsequently corrected; all that we require in this present analysis is the existence of *some* univeral sequence of moral reasoning structures. Even such critics as Gibbs and Gilligan appear to accept this. Such objections must be met if they are well founded, of course, and the *specific* theory of political-social development will change accordingly, but the general approach remains valid.

The third line of defense is the argument that even in the continued absence of any agreement about what moral reasoning looks like, it is nevertheless important to look at conceptions of development for their normative grounding (see Chilton, forthcoming). Even if the nature of morality remains an issue, it is the *right* issue.

For purposes of exposition we assume here that the basic outline of Kohlberg's theory is correct, including also his work on the dynamics of moral reasoning development (and, more broadly, Piaget's work on the dynamics of cognitive development generally).

29   Political development must be located in the cultural system rather than the social system because only within the cultural system can we discuss moral intentions and moral problems. The social system is subject to moral evaluation, but the evaluation derives from other systems; it is not inherent in the social system.

30   Recall the discussion in chapter three of "cooperation" as a fundamentally genetic-epistemological concept.

31   See Kahneman, Slovic, and Tversky (1982). Of course, this latent moral theory is incomplete and would have to be expanded (see note 2 to this chapter).

Bibliography

Achen, C. (1975), "Mass Political Attitudes and the Survey Response," *American Political Science Review*, vol. 69, pp. 1218–1231.

Adelson, J. (1971), "The Political Imagination of the Young Adolescent," *Daedelus*, vol. 100, pp. 1013–1050.

Adelson, J., and R. O'Neil (1966), "The Growth of Political Ideas in Adolescence: The Sense of Community," *Journal of Personality and Social Psychology*, vol. 4, pp. 295–306.

Adelson, J., B. Green, and R. O'Neil (1969), "The Growth of the Idea of Law in Adolescence," *Developmental Psychology*, vol. 1, pp. 327–332.

Adelson, J., and L. Beall (1970), "Adolescent Perspectives on Law and Government," *Law and Society Review*, vol. 2, pp. 495–504.

Adorno, T. W., E. Frenkel-Brunswik, D. Levinson, R. Sanford (1950), *The Authoritarian Personality* (New York: W. W. Norton).

Allport, G. (1935), "Attitudes," in C. M. Murchison (ed.), *Handbook of Social Psychology* (Worchester, Mass.: Clark University Press).

Almond, G. (1956), "Comparative Political Systems," *Journal of Politics*, vol. 18, pp. 391–409.

Almond, G., and S. Verba (1963), *The Civic Culture: Political Attitudes and Democracy in Five Nations* (Princeton, N.J.: Princeton University Press).

Axelrod, R. (1973), "Schema Theory: An Information Processing Model of Perception and Cognition," *American Political Science Review*, vol. 67, pp. 1248–1266.

Bachrach, P., and M. Baratz (1963), "The Two Faces of Power," *American Political Science Review*, vol. 56, pp. 947–952.

Baltes, P., and K. W. Schaie (1973) (eds.), *Life-Span Developmental Psychology* (New York: Academic Press).

Benedict, R. (1946), *The Chrysanthemum and the Sword* (Boston: Houghton Mifflin).

Bennett, L. (1975), *The Political Mind and the Political Environment* (Lexington, Mass.: Lexington Books).

Berti, A. E., A. S. Bombi, and A. Lis (1982), "The Child's Conceptions about Means of Production and Their Owners," *European Journal of Social Psychology*, vol. 12, pp. 21–239.

Berti, A. E., A. S. Bombi, and R. De Beni (1986), "Acquiring Economic Notions: Profit," *International Journal of Behavioral Development*, vol. 9, pp. 15–29.

Best, J. (1973), *Public Opinion: Micro and Macro* (Homewood, Ill.: Dorsey Press).

Bettelheim, B. (1960), *The Informed Heart* (New York: Avon Books).

Binford, M. (1983), "Democratic Political Personality: Functions of Attitudes and Styles of Reasoning," *Political Psychology*, vol. 4, no. 4, pp. 663–684.

Bloch, M. (1961), *Feudal Society: The Growth of Ties of Dependence* and *Social Classes and Political Organization* (Chicago: University of Chicago Press).

Bolland, J., J. Kuklinski, and R. Luskin (1987), "Schema Theory in Political Psychology," paper presented at the annual meeting of the International Society of Political Psychology, San Francisco.

Campbell, A., P. Converse, W. Miller, and D. Stokes (1960), *The American Voter* (New York: Wiley).

Chilton, S. (1977), "The Analysis of Power Structures in Three High Schools" (unpublished Ph.D. diss., MIT).

———. (1988), "Defining Political Culture," *Western Political Quarterly*, vol. 41, no. 3.

———. (1988b), *Defining Political Development* (Boulder, Colo.: Lynne Rienner).

———. (forthcoming), "Any Complete Theory of Social Change Inevitably Incorporates a Normatively Grounded Theory of Moral Choice," *Journal of Developing Societies*.

Colby, A., and L. Kohlberg (1987), *The Measurement of Moral Judgment*, 2 vols. (New York: Cambridge University Press).

Colby, A., L. Kohlberg, J. Gibbs, and M. Lieberman (1983), "A Longitudinal Study of Moral Judgment," *Monograph of the Society for Research in Child Development*, vol. 48, no. 4.

Connell, R. W. (1971), "Bibliography and Review of Findings of Two-Generation Surveys of Political and Social Attitudes," Working Paper 163, Center for Social Organization Studies, University of Chicago.

Converse, P. (1964), "The Nature of Belief Systems in Mass Publics," in D. Apter (ed.), *Ideology and Discontent* (New York: Free Press).

———. (1975), "Public Opinion and Voting Behavior," in F. A. Greenstein and N. Polsby (eds.), *The Handbook of Political Science* (Reading, Mass.: Addison-Wesley).

Cowan, P. (1966), "Cognitive Egocentrism and Social Interaction in Children," *American Psychologist*, vol. 21, p. 623.

Cowan, P., J. Langer, J. Heavenrich, and M. Nathanson (1969), "Social Learning and

Piaget's Cognitive Theory of Moral Development," *Journal of Personality and Social Psychology*, vol. 2, no. 3, pp. 261–274.

Crenson, M. (1971), *The Un-Politics of Air Pollution* (Baltimore: Johns Hopkins University Press).

Dahl, R. (1956), *A Preface to Democratic Theory* (Chicago: University of Chicago Press).

———. (1961), *Who Governs?* (New Haven, Conn.: Yale University Press).

Danet, B. (1971), "The Language of Persuasion in Bureaucracy: 'Modern' and 'Traditional' Appeals to the Israel Customs Authorities," *American Sociological Review*, vol. 36, pp. 847–859.

Dasen, P. (1977), *Piagetian Psychology: Cross-Cultural Contributions* (New York: Halstead Press).

Deutsch, K. W., J. I. Dominguez, and H. Heclo (1981), *Comparative Government: Politics of Industrialized and Developing Nations* (Boston: Houghton Mifflin).

Dittmer, L. (1977), "Political Culture and Political Symbolism: Toward a Theoretical Synthesis," *World Politics*, vol. 29, pp. 552–583.

Doebert, R. (1981), "The Role of Stage Models within a Theory of Social Evolution Illustrated by the European Witch Craze," in U. J. Jensen and R. Harre (eds.), *The Philosophy of Evolution* (Brighton, Sussex: Harvester Press).

Duby, G. (1977), *The Chivalrous Society*, trans. Cynthia Postam (Stanford, Calif.: Stanford University Press).

Easton, D., and R. Hess (1962), "The Child's Political World," *Midwest Journal of Political Science*, vol. 6, pp. 229–246.

Easton, D., and J. Dennis (1965), "The Child's Image of Government," *Annals*, vol. 361, p. 40–57.

Eckstein, H. (1982), "The Idea of Political Development: From Dignity to Efficiency," *World Politics*, vol. 34, pp. 451–486.

Edwards, C. (1975), "Societal Complexity and Moral Development: A Kenyan Study," *Ethos*, vol. 3, pp. 505–527.

Eisenstadt, S. N., and R. Lemarchand (eds.) (1981), *Political Clientalism: Patronage and Development* (Beverly Hills, Calif.: Sage Publications).

Elazar, D. (1966), *American Federalism: A View from the States* (New York: Crowell).

Elias, N. (1978), *The History of Manners* (New York: Pantheon).

———. (1982), *Power and Civility* (New York: Pantheon).

Elkins, D., and R. Simeon (1979), "A Cause in Search of Its Effect, or What Does Political Culture Explain?," *Comparative Politics*, vol. 11, pp. 127–145.

England, D. (1984), "A Reconceptualization of the Nature of Mass Belief Systems," paper presented at annual meeting of the American Political Science Association, Washington, D.C.

Feffer, M. (1959), "The Cognitive Implications of Role-Taking Behavior," *Journal of Personality*, vol. 27, pp. 152–168.

————. (1967), "Symptom Expression as a Form of Primitive Decentering," *Psychological Review*, vol. 174, pp. 152–168.

Feffer, M., and V. Gourevitch (1960), "Cognitive Aspects of Role-Taking in Children," *Journal of Personality*, vol. 28, pp. 384–396.

Feffer, M., and L. Suchotliff (1966), "Decentering Implications of Social Interactions," *Journal of Personality and Social Psychology*, vol. 4, no. 4, pp. 415–422.

Fenno, R., Jr. (1978), *Home Style: House Members in Their Districts* (Boston: Little, Brown).

Field, J., and R. Anderson (1969), "Ideology in the Public's Conception of the 1964 Election," *Public Opinion Quarterly*, vol. 33, pp. 380–398.

Fishkin, J. (1982), *Beyond Subjective Morality* (New Haven, Conn.: Yale University Press).

Fishkin, J., K. Keniston, and K. McKinnon (1973), "Moral Reasoning and Political Ideology," *Journal of Personality and Social Psychology*, vol. 27, pp. 109–119.

Flavell, J. (1963), *The Developmental Psychology of Jean Piaget* (Princeton, N.J.: Van Nostrand).

————. (1966), "Role-Taking and Communication Skills in Children," *Young Children*, vol. 21, pp. 164–177.

Flavell, J., et al. (1968), *The Development of Role-Taking and Communication Skills in Children* (New York: Wiley).

Freud, S. (1953), *The Standard Edition of the Complete Psychological Works* (New York: Hogarth Press).

Frey, F. (1971), "Developmental Aspects of Administration," in J. P. Leagous and C. P. Loomis (eds.), *Behavioral Change in Administration* (Ithaca, N.Y.: Cornell University Press).

Gallatin, J., and J. Adelson (1970), "Individual Rights and the Public Good: A Cross-National Study of Adolescence," *Comparative Political Studies*, vol. 2, pp. 226–244.

Garfinkel, H. (1967), *Studies in Ethnomethodology* (Englewood Cliffs, N.J.: Prentice-Hall).

Gaventa, J. (1980), *Power and Powerlessness* (Urbana: University of Illinois Press).

Geertz, C. (1964), "Ideology as a Cultural System," in D. Apter (ed.), *Ideology and Discontent* (New York: Free Press).

————. (1973), *The Interpretation of Cultures* (New York: Basic Books).

Gibbs, J. (1977), "Kohlberg's Stages of Moral Judgment: A Constructive Critique," *Harvard Educational Review*, vol. 47, pp. 43–61.

Gilligan, C. (1982), *In a Different Voice: Psychological Theory and Women's Development* (Cambridge, Mass.: Harvard University Press).

Graber, D. (1982), "Have I Heard This Before and Is It Worth Knowing: Variations in Political Information Processing," paper presented at the annual meeting of the American Political Science Association, Denver.

Haan, N., M. B. Smith, and J. Block (1968), "Moral Reasoning of Young Adults:

Political-Social Behavior, Family Background, and Personality Correlates," *Journal of Personality and Social Psychology*, vol. 10, no. 3, pp. 183–201.

Habermas, J. (1975), *Legitimation Crisis* (Boston: Beacon Press).

——. (1979), *Communication and the Evolution of Society* (Boston: Beacon Press).

——. (1979a), "What Is Universal Pragmatics?," in Habermas, 1979, pp. 1–68.

——. (1979b), "Historical Materialism and the Development of Normative Structures," in Habermas, 1979, pp. 95–129.

——. (1983), "Interpretive Social Science vs. Hermeneuticism," in N. Haan, R. Bellah, P. Rabinow, and W. Sullivan (eds.), *Social Science as Moral Inquiry* (New York: Columbia University Press).

Hagen, E. (1962), *On the Theory of Social Change: How Economic Growth Begins* (Homewood, Ill.: Dorsey Press).

Hall, A. (1977), "Patron-Client Relations: Concepts and Terms," in S. Schmidt et al., *Friends, Followers, and Factions* (Berkeley: University of California Press), pp. 510–512.

Harvey, O., D. Hunt, and H. Schroder (1961), *Conceptual Systems and Personality Organization* (New York: Wiley).

Hegel, G. W. F. (1975), *Lectures on the Philosophy of World History, Introduction: Reason in History* (New York: Cambridge University Press).

Hess, R. (1963), "The Socialization of Attitudes Toward Political Authority: Some Cross-National Comparisons," *International Social Science Journal*, vol. 15, pp. 542–549.

Hewitt, J. (1979), *Self and Society: A Symbolic Interactionist Social Psychology*, 2d ed. (Boston: Allyn and Bacon).

Higgins, E. T., D. Ruble, and W. Hartup (eds.) (1983), *Social Cognition and Social Development: A Sociocultural Perspective* (New York: Cambridge University Press).

Himmelweit, H., et al. (1981), *How Voters Decide* (New York: Academic Press).

Hobhouse, L. T. (1906), *Morals in Evolution* (London: Chapman and Hall) (1951 reprint).

Hunter, F. (1953), *Community Power Structure* (Chapel Hill: University of North Carolina Press).

Huntington, S. P. (1971), "The Change to Change: Modernization, Development, and Politics," *Comparative Politics*, vol. 3, no. 3, pp. 283–322.

Hyman, H., and P. Sheatsley (1956), "Attitudes toward Discrimination," *Scientific American*, vol. 195, pp. 35–39.

Inhelder, B. (1953), "Criteria of the Stages of Mental Development," in S. Tanner and B. Inhelder (eds.), *Discussion on Child Development* (London: Tavistock), pp. 75–107.

Jackins, H. (1987), "Understanding and Using Organizational Forms," in *The Longer View* (Seattle: Rational Island Publishers).

Jahoda, G. (1959), "The Development of Perception of Social Difference in Children from Six to Ten," *British Journal of Educational Psychology*, vol. 50, pp. 159–175.

———. (1963), "The Development of Children's Ideas About Country and Nationality, Part 1: The Conceptual Framework," *British Journal of Educational Psychology*, vol. 33, pp. 47–60.

———. (1964), "Children's Concepts of Nationality: A Critical Study of Piaget's Stages," *Child Development*, vol. 35, pp. 1081–1092.

Judd, C., and M. Milburn (1980), "Structure of Attitude Systems in the General Public: Comparisons of a Structural Equation Model," *American Sociological Review*, vol. 45, pp. 627–643.

Kahneman, D., P. Slovic, and A. Tversky (1982), *Judgment Under Uncertainty: Heuristics and Biases* (New York: Cambridge University Press).

Katznelson, I. (1973), *Black Men, White Cities* (Oxford: Oxford University Press).

Kemeny, J. (1976), *An Interactionist Approach to Macro Sociology* (Gothenburg, Sweden: University of Gothenburg, Department of Sociology, monograph 10, October).

Kerlinger, F. (1984), *Liberalism and Conservatism: The Nature and Structure of Social Attitudes* (Hillsdale, N.J.: Lawrence Erlbaum Associates).

Kinder, D. (1982), "Enough Already about Ideology: The Many Bases of American Public Opinion," paper presented at the annual meeting of the American Political Science Association, Denver.

Kingdon, J. (1973), *Congressmen's Voting Decisions* (New York: Harper and Row).

Kohlberg, L. (1963), "Moral Development and Identification," in H. Stevenson (ed.), *Child Psychology, 62nd Yearbook of the National Society for the Study of Education* (Chicago: University of Chicago Press).

———. (1963a), "The Development of Children's Orientations toward a Moral Order: I, Sequence in the Development of Moral Thought," *Vita Humana*, vol. 6, pp. 11–33.

———. (1964), "The Development of Moral Character and Ideology," in M. Hoffman and L. Hoffman (eds.), *Review of Child Development Research* (New York: Russell Sage).

———. (1971), "From Is to Ought: How to Commit the Naturalistic Fallacy and Get Away with It in the Study of Moral Development," in T. Mischel (ed.), *Cognitive Development and Epistemology* (New York: Academic Press).

———. (1973), "Continuities in Childhood and Adult Moral Development Revisited," in P. Baltes and K. W. Schaie (eds.), *Life-Span Developmental Psychology* (New York: Academic Press).

———. (1981a), *Essays on Moral Development: Vol. 1, The Philosophy of Moral Development* (San Francisco: Harper and Row).

———. (1981b), "Justice as Reversibility: The Claim to Moral Adequacy of a Highest Stage of Moral Judgment," in Kohlberg, 1981, pp. 190–226.

———. (1981c), "Appendix: The Six Stages of Moral Judgment," in Kohlberg, 1981, pp. 409–412.

———. (1984), *Essays on Moral Development: Vol. II, The Psychology of Moral Development* (San Francisco: Harper and Row).

———. (1984a), "Stage and Sequence: The Cognitive-Developmental Approach to Socialization," in Kohlberg, 1984, pp. 7–169.

———. (1984b), "Appendix A: The Six Stages of Justice Judgment," in Kohlberg, 1984, pp. 621–639.

Kohlberg, L., and D. Candee (1983), "The Relation of Moral Judgment to Moral Action," in W. Kurtines and J. L. Gewirtz (eds.), *Morality, Moral Behavior, and Moral Development,* (New York: Wiley).

Kohlberg, L., and R. Kramer (1969), "Continuities and Discontinuities in Childhood and Adult Moral Development," *Human Development,* vol. 12, pp. 93–120.

Kohlberg, L., C. Levine, and A. Hewer (1984c), "The Current Form of the Theory," in Kohlberg, 1984, pp. 12–319.

———. (1984d), "Synopses and Detailed Replies to Critics," in Kohlberg, 1984, pp. 320–386.

Kuhn, T. (1970a), *The Structure of Scientific Revolutions* (Chicago: University of Chicago Press).

———. (1970b), "Logic of Discovery or Psychology of Research?" and "Reflections on My Critics," in I. Lakatos and A. Musgrave, (eds.), *Criticism and the Growth of Knowledge* (New York: Cambridge University Press).

Lande, C. H. (1977), "Group Politics and Dyadic Politics: Notes for A Theory," in Schmidt et al. (eds.), 1977, pp. 506–510.

Lane, R. (1962), *Political Ideology* (New York: Free Press).

———. (1983), "Political Observers and Market Participants: The Effect on Cognition," *Political Psychology,* vol. 4, no. 3, pp. 455–482.

———. (1986), "What Are People Trying to Do with Their Schemata? The Question of Purpose," in R. Lau and D. Sears (eds.), *Political Cognition* (Hillsdale, N.J.: Lawrence Erlbaum Associates).

LaPalombara, J. (ed.) (1967), *Bureaucracy and Political Development* (Princeton, N.J.: Princeton University Press).

Lau, R., and D. O. Sears (1986), *Political Cognition* (Hillsdale, N.J.: Lawrence Erlbaum Associates).

Le Carré, J. (1977), *The Honourable Schoolboy* (New York: Alfred A. Knopf).

Lehman, E. (1971), "Social Indicators and Social Problems," in E. O. Smigel (ed.), *Handbook on the Study of Social Problems* (Chicago: Rand McNally).

———. (1972), "On the Concept of Political Culture: A Theoretical Reassessment," *Social Forces,* vol. 50, pp. 361–370.

Lijphart, A. (1977), *Democracy in Plural Societies* (New Haven, Conn.: Yale University Press).

Looft, W. (1972), "Egocentrism and Social Interaction Across the Life Span," *Psychological Bulletin,* vol. 78, pp. 73–92.

Looft, W., and D. Charles (1971), "Egocentrism and Social Interaction in Young and Old Adults," *Aging and Human Development,* vol. 2, pp. 21–28.

Lukes, S. (1974), *Power: A Radical View* (London: Macmillan).

Luttbeg, N. (1968), "The Structure of Beliefs Among Leaders and the Public," *Public Opinion Quarterly*, vol. 32, no. 3.

McCarthy, T. (1979), "Translator's Introduction," in J. Habermas, *Communication and the Evolution of Society* (Boston: Beacon Press), pp. vii–xxiv.

McClelland, D. (1976), *The Achieving Society* (New York: Irvington).

Mann, R. (1967), *Interpersonal Styles and Group Development* (New York: Wiley).

Mannoni, O. (1956), *Prospero and Caliban* (New York: Praeger).

Mansbridge, J. (1980), *Beyond Adversary Democracy* (Chicago: University of Chicago Press).

Marx, K., and F. Engels (1848), "The Communist Manifesto," in *Collected Works* (Moscow: Progress Publishers), pp. 477–519.

———. (1975), *Collected Works: Volume Four* (Moscow: Progress Publishers.)

Mendilow, J. (1986), *The Romantic Tradition in British Political Thought* (London: Croom Helm).

Merelman, R. (1966), "The Development of Political Ideology: A Framework for the Analysis of Political Socialization," *American Political Science Review*, vol. 68, no. 3, pp. 750–767.

———. (1984), *Making Something of Ourselves: Culture and Politics in the United States* (Berkeley: University of California Press).

Milgram, S. (1974), *Obedience to Authority* (New York: Harper).

Modgil, S. (1974), *Piagetian Research: Handbook of Recent Studies* (Windsor: NFER).

Neugarten, B. (1949), "Democracy of Childhood," in Warner et al., *Democracy in Jonesville* (New York: Harper).

Nie, N., S. Verba, and J. Petrocik (1976), *The Changing American Voter* (Cambridge, Mass.: Harvard University Press).

Nie, N., and J. Rabjohn (1979), "Revisiting Mass Belief Systems Revisited: Or Doing Research Is Like Watching a Tennis Match," *American Journal of Political Science*, vol. 23, pp. 139–175.

Nisan, M., and L. Kohlberg (1984), "Cultural Universality of Moral Judgment States: A Longitudinal Study in Turkey," in L. Kohlberg, *Essays on Moral Development* (San Francisco: Harper and Row), pp. 582–593.

Overton, W. (1983), *The Relationship between Social and Cognitive Development* (Hillsdale, N.J.: Lawrence Erlbaum Associates).

Parsons, T. (1961), "An Outline of the Social System," in T. Parsons et al. (eds.), *Theories of Society: Foundations of Modern Sociological Theory* (New York: Free Press), pp. 30–79.

Patterson, J. (1975), "Moral Development and Political Thinking: The Case of Freedom of Speech," paper presented at the Psychology and Politics Program Symposium, Yale University, Spring.

Peluffo, N. (1967), "Culture and Cognitive Problems," *International Journal of Psychology*, vol. 2, pp. 187–198).

Pennock, J. R. (1979), *Democratic Political Theory* (Princeton, N.J.: Princeton University Press).

Piaget, J. (1955), *The Language and Thought of the Child* (Cleveland: Meridian Books), originally published in 1923.

———. (1960), *The Psychology of Intelligence* (Totowa, N.J.: Littlefield, Adams,)), originally published in 1947.

———. (1960), *The Child's Conception of the World* (Totowa, N.J.: Littlefield, Adams), originally published in 1926.

———. (1962), "The Stages of Intellectual Development of the Child," *Bulletin of the Menninger Clinic*, vol. 26, no. 3, pp. 120–128.

———. (1963), *The Origins of Intelligence in the Child* (New York: W. W. Norton), originally published in 1936.

———. (1965), *The Moral Judgment of the Child* (New York: Free Press), originally published in 1932.

———. (1968), *Six Psychological Studies* (New York: Vintage), originally published in 1964.

———. (1969), *Judgment and Reasoning in the Child* (Totowa, N.J.: Littlefield, Adams), originally published in 1924.

———. (1969a), *The Child's Conception of Physical Causality* (Totowa, N.J.: Littlefield, Adams), originally published in 1924.

———. (1970), *Genetic Epistemology* (New York: W. W. Norton).

———. (1971), *Biology and Knowledge* (Chicago: University of Chicago Press).

———. (1971a), *Structuralism* (New York: Harper).

———. (1971b), *The Construction of Reality in the Child* (New York: Ballantine), originally published in 1936.

———. (1973), *The Child and Reality* (New York: Viking), originally published in 1972.

———. (1976), *The Grasp of Consciousness* (Cambridge, Mass.: Harvard University Press), originally published in 1974.

———. (1977), *The Development of Thought: Equilibration of Cognitive Structures* (New York: Viking).

———. (1977a), *Etudes Sociologiques* (Geneva: Librairie Droz).

———. (1978), *Success and Understanding* (Cambridge, Mass.: Harvard University Press), originally published in 1974.

Piaget, J., and B. Inhelder (1969), *The Psychology of the Child* (New York: Basic Books), originally published in 1966.

Piaget, J., and A. Weil (1951), "The Development in Children of the Idea of the Homeland and of Relations with Other Countries," *International Social Science Bulletin*, vol. 3, pp. 561–578.

Pirenne, H. (1952), *Medieval Cities: Their Origins and the Revival of Trade* (Princeton, N.J.: Princeton University Press).

Poggi, G. (1978), *The Development of the Modern State: A Sociological Introduction* (Stanford, Calif.: Stanford University Press).

Prince, J. R. (1968), "The Effect of Western Education on Science Conceptualization in New Guinea," *British Journal of Educational Psychology,* vol. 38, pp. 64–74.

Pye, L. (1965), "Introduction: Political Culture and Political Development," in L. Pye and S. Verba (eds.), *Political Culture and Political Development* (Princeton, N.J.: Princeton University Press), pp. 3–26.

———. (1966), "The Concept of Political Development," in Lucian Pye, *Aspects of Political Development* (Boston: Little, Brown), pp. 31–48.

———. (1972), "Culture and Political Science: Problems in the Evaluation of the Concept of Political Culture," *Social Science Quarterly,* vol. 10, pp. 285–296.

Radding, C. (1979), "Superstition to Science: Nature, Fortune, and the Passing of the Medieval Ordeal," *American Historical Review,* vol. 84, pp. 945–969.

———. (1985), *A World Made by Men: Cognition and Society, 400–1200* (Chapel Hill: University of North Carolina Press).

Rawls, J. (1971), *A Theory of Justice* (Cambridge, Mass.: Belknap Press).

Rejai, M. (1967), *Democracy: The Contemporary Theories* (New York: Atherton).

Riegel, K. F., and G. C. Rosenwald (1975), *Structure and Transformation: Developmental and Historical Aspects* (New York: Wiley).

Rokeach, M. (1960), *The Open and Closed Mind* (New York: Basic Books).

Rosenberg, S. W. (1981), "The Developmental Analysis of Political Cognition," paper presented at the annual meeting of the International Society of Political Psychology, Mannheim, West Germany.

———. (1982), "The Structural Developmental Analysis of Political Thinking: An Alternative to the Belief Systems Approach," paper presented at the annual meeting of the American Political Science Association, Denver.

———. (1983), "The Study of Political Ideology: The Validity, Power, and Utility of the Theories We Construct," paper presented at the annual meeting of the International Society of Political Psychology, Oxford, England.

———. (1985), "Sociology, Psychology, and the Study of Political Behavior, *Journal of Politics,* vol. 47, pp. 715–731.

———. (1987), "Reason and Ideology: Interpreting People's Understanding of American Politics," *Polity,* vol. 20, pp. 114–144.

———. (1988a), "The Structure of Political Thinking," *American Journal of Political Science,* vol. 32, pp. 539–566.

———. (1988b), *Reason, Ideology, and Politics* (Princeton, N.J.: Princeton University Press; Cambridge, England: Polity Press).

Ross, L. (1977), "The Intuitive Psychologist and His Shortcomings," in L. Berkowitz (ed.), *Advances in Experimental Social Psychology,* vol. 10 (New York: Academic Press).

Rottenberg, M. (1974), "Conceptual and Methodological Notes on Affective and Cognitive Role-Taking (Sympathy and Empathy)," *Journal of Genetic Psychology,* vol. 125.

Sampson, S. (1978), *Crisis in a Cloister* (Norwood, N.J.: Ablex).

Schelling, T. (1980), *The Strategy of Conflict* (Cambridge, Mass.: Harvard University Press), originally published in 1960.

Schmidt, S., J. Scott, C. Lande, and L. Guasti (eds.) (1977), *Friends, Followers, and Factions: A Reader in Political Clientelism* (Berkeley: University of California Press).

Selman, R. (1971), "The Relation of Role-Taking to the Development of Moral Judgment in Children," *Child Development*, vol. 42, pp. 79–91.

———. (1975), "Taking Another's Perspective: Role-Taking in Early Childhood," *Child Development*, vol. 29, pp. 379–388.

Sheatsley, P., G. Taylor, and A. Greeley (1978), "Attitudes toward Racial Integration," *Scientific American*, vol. 238, pp. 42–49.

Siegal, R. (1970), *Learning About Politics* (New York: Random House).

Sinnott, J. D. (1975), "Everyday Thinking and Piagetian Operativity in Adults," *Human Development*, vol. 18, pp. 430–443.

Smith, E. R. A. N. (1980), "The Levels of Conceptualization: False Measures of Ideological Sophistication," *American Political Science Review*, vol. 74, no. 3, pp. 685–696.

Snarey, J., J. Reimer, and L. Kohlberg (1984), "Cultural Universality of Moral Judgment Stages: A Longitudinal Study in Israel," in L. Kohlberg, *Essays on Moral Development* (San Francisco: Harper and Row), pp. 594–620.

Stimson, J. (1975), "Belief Systems: Constraint, Complexity, and the 1972 Election," *American Journal of Political Science*, vol. 19, pp. 383–418.

Sullivan, J., J. Pierson, and G. Marcus (1978), "Ideological Constraint in the Mass Public: A Methodological Critique and Some New Findings," *American Journal of Political Science*, vol. 22, pp. 233–249.

Taylor, S. E., and S. T. Fiske (1975), "Point of View and the Perceptions of Causality," *Journal of Personality and Social Psychology*, vol. 32, pp. 439–445.

———. (1978), "Salience, Attention and Attribution: Top of the Head Phenomena," in L. Berkowitz (ed.), *Advances in Experimental Social Psychology, Vol. II* (New York: Academic Press).

Taylor, S. E., and J. Crocker (1981), "Schematic Bases of Social Information Processing," in E. T. Higgins, C. P. Herman, and M. P. Zanna (eds.), *Social Cognition: The Ontario Symposium*, vol. 1 (Hillsdale, N.J.: Lawrence Erlbaum Associates).

Tversky, A., and D. Kahneman (1974), "Judgment Under Uncertainty: Heuristics and Biases," *Science*, vol. 185, pp. 1124–1131.

Ungar, R. U. (1975), *Knowledge and Politics* (New York: Free Press).

Verba, S., and N. Nie (1972), *Participation in America* (New York: Harper and Row).

Vygotsky, L. S. (1962), *Thought and Language* (Cambridge, Mass.: MIT Press).

———. (1978), *Mind in Society: The Development of Higher Psychological Processes* (Cambridge, Mass.: Harvard University Press).

Wagner, J. (1984), "Toward New Directions in the Study of Public Opinion: An

Application of Developmental Theory to Survey Research," paper delivered at the annual meeting of the Midwest Political Science Association, Chicago.

Walzer, M. (1977), *Just and Unjust Wars* (New York: Basic Books).

Ward, D. (1981) "Ideology and Generations," unpublished Ph.D. diss., Yale University.

———. (1982), "Genetic Epistemology and the Structure of Belief Systems: An Introduction to Piaget for Political Scientists," paper presented at the annual meeting of the American Political Science Association, Denver; available from ERIC.

Wason, P. C., and P. M. Johnson-Laird (1972), *Psychology of Reasoning: Structure and Content* (Cambridge, Mass.: Harvard University Press).

Weinreich, H. (1977), "Some Consequences of Replicating Kohlberg's Original Moral Development Study on a British Sample," *Journal of Moral Education*, vol. 7, pp. 32–39.

Weschler, J. (ed.) (1978), *On Aesthetics in Science* (Cambridge, Mass.: MIT Press).

White, R. K. (1984), *Fearful Warriors* (New York: Free Press).

White, H., S. Boorman, and R. Breiger (1975), "Social Structure from Multiple Networks: I. Blockmodels of Roles and Positions," *American Journal of Sociology*, vol. 81, no. 4, pp. 730–780.

Wolin, S. (1960), *The Politics of Vision: Continuity and Innovation in Western Political Thought* (Boston: Little, Brown).

Wray, J. (1979), "Comment on Interpretations of Early Research into Belief Systems," *Journal of Politics*, vol. 41, pp. 1173–1181.

Wright, T. (1984), "The First Ibañez Administration in Chile (1927–1931): A Preliminary Assessment," paper presented at the annual meeting of the Rocky Mountain Council on Latin American Studies, Tucson, Arizona, February 23–25, 1984.

Youniss, J. (1978), "Dialectical Theory and Piaget on Social Knowledge," *Human Development*, vol. 21, pp. 234–247.

Zellerman, G., and D. O. Sears (1971), "Childhood Origins of Tolerance for Dissent," *Journal of Social Issues*, vol. 27, no. 2, pp. 109–136.

Index